# the DEPARTMENT
# that doesn't exist

### a true story

## Helen   Jay   Hamilton

# Acknowledgements

A heartfelt thanks to my four children, who all stood by me during the writing of this book and offered valuable feedback. They listened to me patiently, were always so encouraging, and even became excited as the jigsaw began to fall into place for them as well.

I owe a special thanks to my editor, Linda Lloyd, for her patience and belief in the book, and her dedicated work on it.

Of course, to my dear, dear friend Jessie, who, after all these years, is still with me. Even when she no longer is in body, she will continue to be in spirit.

Finally, to Peter, whose memory I still carry gently in my heart.

# Contents

# Prologue

It was always whispered that there was a secret Department deep inside the British Intelligence Services, known only to a few select people. If spoken of at all it was referred to as 'the Department that does not exist'.

Quite a few people had heard about it, but not many actually believed in it. After all, how could there be such a thing? It was obviously just an excuse, a ploy to try and hide the shame of the leaks and moles, the betrayals and defections of people such as Burgess and Maclean.

There was no truth in it, they said.

I say that is not so. 'The Department that does not exist' certainly did, yet, paradoxically, there was no Department. There were no employers or employees, no contracts or salaries, no buildings, files or records.

I know because I was there.

I have written this book because I believe this is a story that needs to be told, for it is part of the history of Great Britain. The reader must be left to make his or her own judgement as to its veracity. The cognoscenti will know the truth but of course they will be silent – or they will be vociferous in their denial.

I was one of the cognoscenti but I didn't choose to be involved. I was thrown into it. Because of my youth and naivety I suddenly found myself right there at the very seat of power.

However, this is not a book about the Department. That is still shrouded in secrecy, as it must be. This book is a love story.

It is about a man, a remarkable and extraordinary

Englishman. I want the world to know the story of this man who created and ran the Department from its inception in the early 1950s until his death over twenty years later. I want them to see him through my eyes. All those years ago, I found myself right beside him, caught up in the middle of it all. In the process I fell in love with him and the things he stood for.

I believed in him, in everything he told me and everything I saw.

When you have read this book you may ask yourself whether you believe it. It may be better for the world to presume it is fiction, but I don't think so.

Whether you believe it or not, I want it to leave you with hope: hope that something like that could exist; that hundreds of ordinary yet extraordinary men and women of valour could work and fight for everything that was finest and best in this country of ours. I was and still am full of admiration for everything I witnessed.

What I do not want is for this book to endanger or expose anyone or anything that happened at that time. For me it is imperative that no damage is done, so I have waited over thirty years to write it.

The things I saw and heard were of profound importance, not only to Great Britain but to the West. I am convinced that the Department was essential to the security of the whole of the free world. The Cold War was at its height. The danger of Russian aggrandisement was very real. The official Intelligence Services had been infiltrated and no-one was sure to what extent.

This book is about everything that is great in Great Britain. It challenges the constant ridiculing of our Intelligence Services. They were the best in the world then, and I'm sure they still are today.

In these times of political squalor, sleaze and denigration of our country, this is a story that I hope will lift people out of the abyss of national despair, back into a belief in honour, integrity, loyalty, respect and patriotism – words that are, in Britain today, so often derided and scorned. Yet I believe these are values still deeply yearned for by the majority of British people. We long to return to a time when men of honour, truth and integrity were admired and considered heroes; and when such men were the norm. These values are still in our character. We just have to believe in them again.

The men and women involved in the Department's work were ordinary people from ordinary places with unremarkable names and everyday jobs. They were also noble knights in shining armour serving their country and sometimes performing deeds of immense courage.

They were led by a man who was quintessentially English, a modern day King Arthur. They were a part of Camelot. If you had been there at that time and had been invited to answer the call, perhaps you too would have found yourself responding to a deep primeval instinct from the well of your British soul. You too might have gone on living your life as normal, knowing that from time to time you would be called upon to mount your white charger, ride out and defend this great country of ours. Perhaps a member of your family, a neighbour or a friend was one of them. If so, they will never tell you.

But thirty years after I took part in these remarkable events, *I* am now ready to tell *my* story.

## Chapter 1
## The Disclosure

Having an affair with Peter, a millionaire playboy eighteen years my senior, was incongruous to my life, yet in a strange way it seemed to fit. I was in my mid-twenties with two children, divorced from a violent, alcoholic husband. Though I did not consider myself beautiful – attractive, yes – having this sophisticated, cultured and incredibly good-looking man in my life had given me the confidence and self-assurance that are normally the preserve of truly exquisite women. I was happy, but only because I was with him.

I was the product of a typical upper-middle-class English background with a father in trade, which, as far as my peers were concerned, placed me somewhere between acceptable and unacceptable. Being in trade was derided, yet my father's success had brought us wealth and privilege. This left me insecure and somewhat uncertain of my position in the world, a feeling heightened by my having married someone my parents considered socially beneath us. Now that marriage was over and I was concerned about the future for myself and my children.

I believed in destiny but nothing in my life previously could have prepared me for what was about to happen that autumn day in the 1960s.

We were driving to Heathrow Airport. Peter was off to America again. I was to take his car back to London for him, then I was going to stay with my friends, Geoff and Alicia, at their mews flat in Belgravia.

But something was bothering me. Two days earlier I had been with a great family friend. She was forty years older than me, and although we were not actually related, we loved each other like grandmother and grandchild.

That day we were deep in one of our favourite pastimes – looking at her old black and white photographs. Jessie had led a fascinating life and I loved looking at all the pictures that recorded it. I would sit and listen to her stories for hours, entranced.

She was telling me about her time in India during the Second World War when the phone rang, so she went to answer it in the hall. The photos were spilled over her coffee table and as I glanced down, there in front of me was a photograph of four people sitting at a table: Jessie, another woman and two men – one of whom was the man now sitting next to me in the car.

When Jessie came back into the room, she sat down and continued where she had left off. But I was no longer listening. I was staring open-mouthed at the photograph. In it, Jessie looked about forty-five and was clearly with the man her own age. Peter and the other woman looked much younger. Turning the photo over, I read on the back 'The Society. London'. I looked more closely. He was much younger, but yes, it was definitely him.

Jessie had stopped talking. The photograph was still in my hand.

'What have you got there, Helen darling?' she asked.

'I don't know.' I showed her. 'Who are these people with you, Jessie? The men are so attractive!'

She laughed and agreed. 'Yes, gorgeous – especially the younger one. But of course, he was much too young for me!'

'Tell me about them,' I said eagerly.

'Well, they were both officers in the RAF. This one

was my friend,' she said, pointing to the older man. 'I only met the younger one – the *really* handsome one – that one night.'

She told me what she knew about him. The name was different. The story was different.

I listened, checking that she was sure about the name. Then I said nothing. I don't know why, as I usually told Jessie everything. Yet something warned me to keep quiet.

Now the photograph was in my handbag and I was plucking up courage to question the man I had always known as Peter.

I looked across at him. He was concentrating on the road, his grey eyes staring straight ahead of him, his mouth a mixture of cruelty and humour. The delicious dimples that appeared when he smiled were missing. There was a hardness to his face now. His hands gripped the wheel of the powerful car as he guided it through the creeping fog.

'My flight may be cancelled,' he said abruptly.

I hope so, I thought; then we could go back together to his beautiful house in Belgravia. Perhaps he would take me for dinner to the Mirabelle, or the Rib Room at the Carlton Towers. Or maybe he would get his butler to serve us something at home. We could listen to the classical music he so loved. Perhaps tonight I could get a little more behind the enigma of the man, the person I glimpsed from time to time behind the steely grey eyes.

At this moment, he was more of an enigma than ever

Peter had told me that he worked for a travel company, travelling the world and inspecting hotels, villas, airlines, cruise ships, providing the company with accurate data, information and assessments. He spoke about it somewhat vaguely, saying it was really just a way of keeping boredom at bay as he did not need the money. The money part appeared to be true, but for someone who referred to his job in such a casual way, his near obsession with work and his absolute perfectionism were strange, to say the least.

'Can I ask you something?' I heard myself say.

'Yes?' He sounded irritable.

'Why do you say you're Peter Royce when actually you are Edward Harper?'

He visibly stiffened, his eyes narrowed as he gripped the wheel tighter. The knuckles of his hands went white. The words hung in the air between us. It seemed time had stopped, and then didn't know where to go. It felt very cold suddenly. The silence grew in volume and intensity.

Eventually he spoke. 'What made you say that?' His voice was even, which disturbed me more than the anger I had been expecting.

Suddenly I was afraid, though I could not put my finger on why. I could not stop talking. I blurted out about the photograph and the story Jessie had told me.

The car pulled into a lay-by and he switched off the engine. There was a silence. He turned to face me.

'Did you say anything to your friend?' The voice was as cold as the eyes that now seemed to bore into my brain. My hands were clammy.

'No, nothing,' I murmured.

'Have you said anything to anyone else?'

'No.'

He stared ahead. The silence became unnerving. I desperately wanted to say something, anything – but what?

Suddenly Peter switched on the ignition and drove back onto the road. He swung the car round and turned back towards London, his foot hard down on the accelerator.

I sat there in silence. Then, hesitantly, I spoke. 'What's wrong?'

'Shut up!'

I stared at him in shock. He was white with what I presumed to be rage.

Oh God! I thought. What have I done?

I reflected on what he had told me about himself. This man was incredibly rich, that was for sure, but beyond that, what did I really know about him? Very little. He never talked about his past, or his childhood. He never referred to his parents or any family. I didn't know if he'd ever been married or had children; or, indeed, if he was married now.

I didn't question him for the same reason I had not questioned Jessie. Something warned me not to.

Although we were having an affair, Peter never let me stay overnight with him. He rarely showed his feelings, but when he did they were intense. He seemed to have absolute control over himself, yet I knew and had seen the tightly-coiled spring that could unwind swiftly and with devastating effect.

We reached London and drove past Harrods in Knightsbridge before turning into Park Lane. The fog had by now turned into smog and the noise of the windscreen wipers tangoed with my thoughts. We had only gone a short distance when Peter swung off right into a maze of back streets. Without warning he turned down a slip-way into an undergrond garage. He flicked off his lights twice and the doors closed behind him.

'Get out and follow me,' he commanded as he led me to a short flight of steps, past two men who sprang to attention.

'Good afternoon, sir,' they said. He nodded curtly in reply.

We entered a small hall with a lift. Peter held the door open for me, then it clanged shut and we were travelling upwards. I did not notice how many floors.

My mind was too full, running around wild with fear like a rabbit trapped in a pen with a fox.

The lift stopped and I followed him along a corridor, into a room.

'Wait here.' He left and I heard a key turn in a lock.

I looked around. The room was bare except for two wooden chairs. The walls were brick except for one, which was a long, horizontal mirror. I went over and looked at myself. The face looking back was pale, vulnerable and frightened.

Suddenly, I felt very alone. Who would know I was here? No-one. Since I had found the photograph, I had not confided in anyone. The people who knew Peter knew him as just that. As far as I could tell, nobody was aware of this other identity I had just discovered.

True, I had told Jessie from the beginning that I was having an affair with a man called Peter. She was always the first to know anything about me. I knew her to be discreet, trusted that she would never tell anyone. I had always been able to trust her.

Jessie had seen the problems in my marriage and knew how unhappy I was. She lived very close to us and always baby-sat for me. After my divorce, she would look after the children, who adored her, when I went to see Peter. She never asked questions, but waited patiently for me to confide in her. I knew she worried about my 'wealthy London playboy', though she never criticised, just gently told me to be careful, that she didn't want me to be hurt again. I was rarely away overnight at this stage. If I was, I always rang her at the end of the day to check on and speak to the children.

Now I was worried – what would she think if I didn't ring tonight?

I had also told Geoff and Alicia about Peter, but

they were almost part of my world with him anyway. I had met Alicia during a short spell as a fashion model after leaving school. She was special to me. Alicia thought that my relationship with Peter was splendid and had encouraged me in it enthusiastically. Until I met him, I had always seen her and Geoff as separate from my normal life, and been a little in awe of their outré, millionaire lifestyle. But they had both been overwhelmingly supportive, and great friends to me.

When I met Peter they were the obvious people to turn to. I had no experience of how to handle someone like him. Geoff and Alicia were good people, they lived in London and they understood the world Peter moved in. They were so pleased for me to have found some happiness, for Geoff had long been worried about the violence in my marriage. He knew that my husband André was always full of remorse afterwards but he had been afraid that one day André's loss of control might kill me.

My life now seemed to straddle two worlds: the rather mundane life of a divorced woman with two small children to care for, and the secret world of glamour, wealth and privilege I inhabited with Peter. I kept them totally separate and surprised myself that I was able to do so.

Whenever I boarded the train for London I became the girl from the glamorous world of modelling, the girl from a wealthy background who was at ease in this sphere of privilege, happy to be travelling towards the man she loved.

One day I was sitting on the train, thrilled at the thought of being with Peter again for a few days. I was wearing a Russian-style black coat with black boots and a bright red scarf wrapped round my neck. The woman opposite kept staring at me, and when she realised I had noticed, she said, 'I hope you don't mind me saying this but you remind me of Anna Karenina going to meet her lover.'

'Well, maybe I am!' I said gently.

Little did she know.

On my return home, I would sink into the acceptance of my failed marriage to a man from an entirely different world, convincing myself that that was where I really belonged. The edges of my two worlds never overlapped or even seemed to blur.

This discrepancy was emphasised even more by my financial situation at that time. I had grown up enjoying a lifestyle afforded by money, but I was never allowed too much of my own. My father disapproved of young people with a lot of cash to throw around. He wisely realised how too much money can corrupt young people, creating a life with no challenge. He wanted my brother and I to realise and appreciate the value of things. However, he did promise us that if we had not smoked before our twenty-first birthdays, he would give us each £100 – a considerable sum in those days. (Incidentally, we both manged it and neither of us has ever smoked.)

The school I attended believed that girls didn't need a serious career. We were expected to go to a Swiss finishing school, or 'do the season' in London before marrying well. When I left I became rebellious, refusing both the finishing school and the season in London. I wanted to do something meaningful with my life.

Deprived of that chance, I reluctantly agreed to do a course at Lucy Clayton, a modelling and charm school for young ladies. At the end, much to my surprise, they actually took me on their books and I did some modelling. My father did not approve and he was right. I quickly became bored with it. It was intellectually sterile. I did, however, make a lot of money, which my father sensibly put into the bank for me until I had enough to buy my first car

In the end I did go to Switzerland – though not to

a finishing school. I went to the International School in Geneva where I was supposed to perfect my French. Instead I met André, a Frenchman working in the hotel trade as a head-waiter. After a year, he came back to England with me and we were married ten days after my twenty-first birthday. Unsurprisingly, my parents were not happy – and not just about his social status. They were also concerned about his heavy drinking. Naively, I thought I could change him.

It was not long before things became financially very difficult. I was no longer modelling, my savings were dwindling and we were trying to live on a waiter's salary. But André drank most of that away.

My father's supportiveness didn't surprise me. He ensured I had the trappings of security: a house, a car, even holidays, which continued after my divorce. I enjoyed a modest degree of comfort, all generously supplied by my father, but it was not the wealth I had grown to expect in my childhood.

When I met Peter, everything had changed. I was transported from my unexceptional situation into the complete opulence of his life. No wonder I felt like two different people.

This ability to be two quite separate characters was to become incredibly important to me in the years that followed. It was a skill I acquired quite naturally, and one that I shared with everyone else involved in the incredible events that overtook my life.

I looked at my watch. It was three o'clock. How long would I be here? I sat down on one of the chairs and tried to herd my thoughts into some kind of order.

Of course this was all a misunderstanding. Soon Peter would come back into the room. He would smile again and explain everything to me. Then we could leave.

Yet something told me this would not happen. I

think I sensed even then that events were unravelling and decisions were being made somewhere else in this building, which would have life-changing repercussions for me. I shivered, though it was not cold.

During the next two hours, until the door opened and Peter walked in, I relived every second of our relationship, playing each one back again and again in my mind in a frantic search for clues.

## Chapter 2
## The Meeting

Two years earlier my husband André and I had flown to Marbella in Southern Spain for a holiday in a luxury hotel. From the beginning, it was clear the trip was going to be a disaster. As André's drinking increased, I had spent most of the time walking on eggshells, trying to placate him.

At five o'clock one evening, he insisted on having yet another drink before we went upstairs to change for dinner. We were sitting at the bar arguing when suddenly there was a stir as people turned to look at something.

The man walking across the marble entrance hall towards us was undoubtedly stunning and he knew it. He also knew how to make an entrance. The air seemed to crackle with unseen lightning as he moved through it with a tensile grace which suggested controlled violence – bottled, frightening.

A woman turned to the barman and said, 'Who's that? Is he a film star?'

The barman laughed. 'No, that is Peter Royce. He is a millionaire playboy. He's just fly in from St Tropez in his private jet. Be careful,' he added to the woman's husband, 'he is looking for talent because he no find there!'

As the man came closer, I studied him. He was around six feet tall, perhaps late thirties, immaculately dressed in a pale grey suit. He was followed by three other men who seemed to be some kind of entourage. When he came up to the bar, I immediately became aware of an almost arrogant sensuality that seemed to emanate from him. There was a feeling of physical tension about him; his presence literally invaded all the space around him.

He spoke in fluent Spanish and the barman appeared to know him. When their drinks were served, he went to sit with the other men at a nearby table.

I suddenly felt self-conscious of what I was wearing, how I was sitting. I could feel his eyes on me. Every time I looked, he was staring at me. I realised without questioning it that I was unbelievably attracted to him. It was as if someone had thumped me hard in the stomach. It felt dangerous.

At that moment André decided to get angry. He turned and said something to me. His words were slurred. Then he grabbed me by the arm, pushed me off the bar-stool and tried to march me towards the stairs, his voice raised.

The humiliation was excruciating. I knew everyone, including Peter Royce, was watching. I saw him make some comment to one of the others, and I wanted to just disappear. Pausing to regain my dignity and confidence, I walked out past his table. His eyes followed me. I tried not to look at him and failed. There was a sardonic grin on his face. I thought I hated him.

We had five more days left of our holiday. All my energy was going into keeping André happy, but quietly I was studying Peter Royce at every opportunity. I realised that almost every woman there, single and attached, was openly chasing him, but no-one got close. He knew how to keep women at bay. In the evenings he would dance and flirt with them but would always return to his own group. He was steely and unapproachable and I quietly wondered what it would take to get behind his mask.

Aware that he was always watching me, I tried to keep myself in the background, but this became impossible when André wanted to dance – the one thing we did extremely well together. We had worked out a sequence of modern dance and, immodest though it may sound, we must have been exciting to watch – André with his dark good looks, me with my blonde hair, striking features and tall, slender figure. Mini-skirts were all the rage and I knew that, as he swung me round, my short full skirt would dance up around my long thighs. Many a night in Marbella we had managed to clear the floor as people craned to watch us and at the end they would clap and ask for more.

Peter Royce never clapped. He would sit there silently, watching our every move – *my* every move. Conscious of this, I began to dance for him.

It was the dancing that caused all the trouble on our final night.

André and I were sitting at a table when the band began to play what the other holidaymakers had christened 'our' dance tune. It was called 'Cuando Sali de Cuba' and the sensuous rhythm of the music matched our style completely. But André was already so inebriated, dancing that night was out. Unfortunately, the other guests did not realise there was a problem, and they tried to pull us onto the floor.

Misinterpreting their enthusiasm, André got up, fists flailing, and knocked me off my chair. There was a shocked silence; even the band faltered, then stopped. Time was suspended and I sensed everyone watching and waiting.

Although I was stunned from the blow, all the restraint of my strict English upbringing came into play. As André swayed on his feet, I got up, smoothed down my skirt and said loudly and clearly, 'André, I'm quite tired. Let's go upstairs.'

I walked across the dance floor, past the bar, along

13

the swimming pool, trying all the time to remember: 'Keep your head up, walk like a lady, don't let yourself down, don't let anyone see that you're hurting.'

Once out of sight, I fled upstairs with André following. Inside the bedroom, he let rip with his frustration and rage, lashing out at me with his fists. Dazed from a punch to my chin, I nevertheless managed to stagger to the door, run out and stumble down the stairs. André did not follow.

In the marbled hall, I stood shaking, wondering where to go. I had to get out of the hotel. As I reached the huge plateglass doors and began to push them open, a hand grasped my shoulder and a cold, clipped voice said, 'I wouldn't if I were you. It's not safe for a woman alone at night in Marbella.'

I turned in surprise. It was Peter Royce. I found myself looking into clear, steel-grey eyes.

'Come with me,' he said. It did not occur to me to question him.

He led me into a small private lounge under the stairs.

'Stay here. You need a drink. Here, take this.'

He pulled a silk handkerchief from the top pocket of his white dinner jacket. I took it automatically, suddenly conscious that something was running down my face. When I looked down at my dress I saw it was blood. My nose was bleeding and now I felt a sharp pain in my chin.

Oh God, I thought.

'Here, drink this.' He was back, pushing a brandy goblet into my hand. 'Your husband is an alcoholic. He's violent. Unless he stops drinking, he may kill you. You will have to leave him. Do you have any children?'

'Yes, I have a child.'

'Then you have a responsibility outside yourself. Leave him.'

I stared at him, shocked at his straight talking. The eyes were impenetrable.

He continued, 'Where were you planning to go?'

'I was going down to the beach. I wanted to walk, wait until he went to sleep.'

'Do you still want to go?'

'Yes.'

'Okay, wait here. I'll get you a passkey and check on your husband. Then I'll come with you. In the meantime, I suggest you go to the cloakroom and tidy up.' He left.

I realised this was a man used to being obeyed. But why was he so cold? Why didn't he smile, even as he showed kindness? And why, in spite of his coldness, did I feel safe in his presence?

It never occurred to me to wonder how he could obtain a passkey, just like that. It never occurred to me not to do as he said.

I went to the cloakroom and tidied myself up as best I could. I sponged my dress without much success and decided it was probably ruined. My nose stopped bleeding and, except for a scratch on my cheek and the beginnings of a large bruise on my chin, I appeared to be okay.

Normally I could avoid the blows as, in his drunken state, André lacked co-ordination and the violence would be over quickly. Tonight had been different, and I felt sick at the thought of what might have happened if I had not managed to escape.

Outside the cloakroom, Peter was waiting.

'He's passed out across the bed. I've removed his shoes. Shall we go?'

I nodded.

We walked towards the beach. The night was still warm, but without the intensity of the sun it was a more soothing warmth – exactly what I needed. My eyes soon adjusted to the dark. We did not speak, but

I felt at ease with this man. He knew the situation and that was a relief. Here was someone with whom I did not have to pretend. I realised that his lack of emotion when he had spoken to me in the hotel was oddly comforting. It was an acceptance of the facts. I needed someone to tell me the truth about my life and no-one ever had until now. The surprise for me was that it should be this aloof stranger.

He walked at least five yards away from me, keeping his distance as if he did not want to be too close to me in any way. Halfway along the beach I took off my sandals, hooked them over my arm and paddled in the water. He did not join me. As we reached the far end, the sand changed into dunes. I stopped at the water's edge and looked out across the sea. Then, as I relaxed, the tears began to flow. I stood looking at the lapping water until I felt more controlled.

At what point did I realise that I wanted him? Was it when I kicked off my sandals and paddled? Was it as I gazed out over the sea, tears pouring down my face? Or was it long before all of that, when he first walked into the hotel? I knew he had been watching me from the start; had I been subconsciously trying to attract him?

Perhaps it was when I turned to face him now. Certainly it was at this point that I recognised for the first time in my life that desire for a man could be overwhelming. It was primeval. I knew I could not stop whatever was about to happen.

He had climbed to the top of one of the sand dunes and was watching me. I waited but he said nothing. I learned later that Peter was never afraid of silence. He recognised its strength.

We looked at one another and I heard myself say, as if from somewhere else, 'I'll do whatever you say.'

'Will you?' he said quietly.

'Yes.'

'Then come here.'

I walked towards him and as I did so I watched him uncoil like a spring, not slowly, subtly, but with one fluid movement, like a genie escaping from its lamp. Suddenly he was really *there*. Fire had replaced ice. I was behind the mask. The eyes were no longer cold, they were glowing like burning charcoal, bright with power and heat.

We made love. It was inevitable. Nothing could have stopped either of us. He was gentle to begin with, kissing away my tears. Then, as I responded, he became insistent, forceful and controlling. I went where he led me, into a place I had never been before. I let myself go and allowed him to take me through. I felt safe. I trusted him.

Walking back afterwards, I thought that I would trust this man with my life. Little did I know, soon I would be required to do just that.

My judgement of him that night was sound, and I trusted him to the day he died and beyond.

When we got back to the hotel I knew I wouldn't sleep. Anyway, André and I were due to leave for the airport at 4 am to catch our flight back to England, so I bathed, changed and threw away my dress, which by now was definitely ruined. After I had packed, I woke André, who finally dressed and took the cases downstairs. We waited in the hall for the bus that would take us to the airport. André said nothing about the previous evening; I doubted he even remembered, and as I had covered my bruises with make-up, there was nothing to remind him of his outburst.

And so I left Marbella but took home my memories of that night with Peter Royce.

I did not see him again for over a year.

Peter had great difficulty in expressing his emotions

17

verbally. He could do so more easily through music and in the early days of our relationship he would give me records with certain parts or songs highlighted on the sleeve to show how he felt. So when, years later, he sent me a tape on which he actually spoke of his feelings, it was the most valuable thing he ever gave me because he gave me himself. In it, he described what happened for him on the beach in Marbella that night.

*'I remember you standing rigid, tears on your cheeks like raindrops. Through all my nerves I felt your wild reckless desire for me, the desire to be held close, to be comforted. I felt the nearness complete. God, the memory of the leap my heart gave when you said, "I will do whatever you say."*

*'My mind and body clamoured for the slim, smouldering girl before me on the beach – the slender beauty of your figure stunned me. I loved your freshness, your simple, direct honest look, the warmth of your eyes. When you walked towards me you seemed caught up in a special light of moon, willow slender, your pale soft skin glowing in the moonwash, the gold of your hair haloed. Like a Goddess of the Maize, a pagan child of sun and thunder. No-one but you was ever enough after that night. Even if the immediate hunger of the flesh was appeased I yearned for you out of older, deeper hungers, things I sensed in you – the warmth of the sun, the peace as deep as time.'*

After that night everything changed for me. It was as if Peter had injected me with some of his confidence and strength.

A few nights after we got back to England, André hit our young daughter. I walked out of the house with my child, never to return. It took me six months to get my divorce, and it was acrimonious and messy, but with Jessie's support I never wavered. I surprised not only myself but others around me.

Three months after my divorce, I gave birth to Peter's son. Part of me tried to deny it was his child; I didn't want to believe it. But part of me knew it was true. Alcohol made André incapable most of the time and we had not made love at all during the Marbella trip. Another part of me was thrilled.

The following autumn, Peter walked back into my life.

I had heard nothing from him since that night in Spain and I had no way of contacting him; I didn't even know where he came from. Sometimes it felt as if that night had just been a mirage; only his silk handkerchief stained with my own blood compelled me to believe it had really happened.

Then, one day, the doorbell rang and there he stood.

You will probably think it strange that I questioned so little about Peter, and it probably was. Yet it never occurred to me to ask him how he knew how to find me, especially as I had moved house and changed my name. I never asked him why he had contacted me after a year, or how he knew I was divorced. None of those questions entered my head at the sight of him. I was just stunned to see him standing there.

'Hello, Helen.' Slowly he walked towards me and everything I had felt that night on the beach returned with double force. I saw again his lean, muscular body, the hard masculine features. I heard again the deep timbre of his low, strong voice. I responded to him in an almost electrical way, for he had magnetism – call it animal or sexual, if you will. He was acutely aware of his attractiveness and that made him doubly dangerous. I could not help responding. I felt as if I had been waiting for him all my life and it was the most natural thing in the world.

'I've come to take you out to lunch.'

I didn't know what to say. I wasn't even sure at that moment that I could speak at all. It was as if the months in between had never been.

He laughed.

Of course I went with him, telling the housekeeper I would be back for the children's bath-time.

The lunch was enjoyable, though somewhat formal, and afterwards he brought me back home and left. He never touched me, not even when he said goodbye.

'I'll phone you next week,' was all he said as he drove away.

I was puzzled and vaguely disappointed. I knew I should be pleased that he hadn't just taken advantage of me, and part of me was. The other part wished that he had. I had been without a man for almost a year, and I now realised it was because he was the only man I wanted. Now he was here, but did not seem to want me.

In the next few weeks a routine developed. Peter never came to the house again; I didn't want him to. I wanted to keep him separate from my children – especially my younger one, his son. I decided immediately not to tell him this was his child. I don't know why, but some protective instinct told me to keep quiet. I was afraid at first that he might ask me about my new baby, but he never showed the slightest interest in either of the children.

He would phone and arrange a meeting somewhere, usually for lunch in a restaurant, but occasionally for a walk. We talked endlessly about so many things. We found we had mutual interests, especially in the worlds of music and literature. We talked about political issues, world events, current affairs. I found him easy to talk to, very knowledgeable, and he seemed genuinely interested in my views. He asked me about my background and childhood – but I sensed a withdrawal when I tried to do the same, so I stopped. He was always the perfect gentleman but there was something unreachable, untouchable about him.

We usually met once a week and I began to live for each meeting. They became the focal point of my week.

But after every time, I felt more and more confused, and deeply sad. He never touched me or showed any sign that he wanted to. I wanted him so badly it physically hurt. Sometimes when I looked at him I was sure it showed in my eyes. I yearned for him but he never responded. It was as if I didn't exist for him in that way. Yet I remembered the night on the beach and I didn't understand.

One day we were having lunch in a suite at the Midland Hotel in Manchester. I suppose by this time I had reluctantly accepted the situation and was prepared to settle for his friendship.

Looking at my watch I realised it was time for me to leave. 'I must go,' I said. 'Thanks for another lovely lunch.'

Peter got up and helped me on with my coat. 'Can you meet me here again next Thursday?'

'Yes,' I said without hesitation. By this time I think I would have gone to the moon with him if he had asked.

'Good. And when you come... ' he paused and looked at me. His eyes narrowed slightly. '...I shall make love to you.'

I was shocked – it was so cold, so clinical, after all these weeks. It sounded as if he was making an appointment.

'Then I won't come,' I heard myself say.

He smiled. 'Oh yes you will,' he said, holding the door open for me. I could think of nothing to say and I left.

Driving home, I kept shaking my head in hurt and disbelief. It was incomprehensible. Was this man just a complete bastard, nothing more? I couldn't believe that either.

The next few days I spent in turmoil. I didn't want to go, yet I knew I wouldn't be able to stop myself. Conflicting emotions careered around in my head, banging up against each other: anger, hurt, fascination, simple curiosity.

Thursday morning came and I went like a lamb to the slaughter. When Peter saw me he just smiled and took me upstairs, drawing me into the luxurious room he had booked for this very purpose.

That was the start of it.

The next few months were really living. I experienced another human being, he experienced me and we didn't need to talk about it. Gradually, very gradually, somewhere deep inside me I began to understand him, if only a little.

He could be so cold, almost glacial, then the coldness would vanish and he would just seem remote. But this remoteness allowed me a certain distance to view him with more clarity. Once or twice I sensed an inexplicable vulnerability and I wondered what had happened to make him throw up his impenetrable shield. Had he been hurt?

It was inevitable that I would fall in love with him.

I knew Peter was also falling in love with me, but it was reluctantly. I made him feel vulnerable and that did not please him.

'I'm a ruthless man, Helen,' he said one day. 'I use people. Sometimes they get hurt. Is that a risk you want to take?'

'Do anything you like, girl, just don't bore me,' he threw at me another time when I innocently asked him if I could look at something.

There were times when he fought our emerging love so hard, his iciness and cruelty were hard to bear and impossible to comprehend. But, since I knew the warmth behind the mask when the spring uncoiled, there were also bursts of incredible happiness such as I had never experienced before. I was enthralled.

I never wondered where our relationship was going; I just knew I had never been closer to life.

There were weeks when I didn't see him, as he said he was travelling with his job. Then the phone would ring, I would hear his voice in the distance – Europe, America, the Far East – and he would tell me what time his flight was due to arrive and where.

I would drop everything and rush to be with him, sometimes just for a few hours. Very occasionally we would have two or three days together, then another airport, another goodbye.

He never let me stay the night with him. If he came to Cheshire that was fine, because I would go home to the children. But two or three times during that year he invited me to go to London, and then I had to stay overnight with Geoff and Alicia.

Although I never questioned Peter, when I was alone I did ask myself questions. I knew it didn't fit, that there was more. But I was afraid to find out. When I was with him everything was in vivid technicolour. When he left it was shades of grey. Even the pain had colour, purple and mauve, but colour. I couldn't bear to go back to the drabness.

So why, but why, had I now chosen to question him?

In my childhood, whenever anything frightened me, it fascinated me in equal measure. There were times even at this early stage when Peter frightened me, and so I would become more fascinated. I wanted so much to know him more, to understand him more. Naively, I thought that if only I could make him happy, the distance and cruelty would stop.

This didn't happen, but instead of turning me away from him it just made me more determined to reach him.

When I saw the photograph and found out that

Peter was not the person he said he was, my heart leapt. Here, finally, was something I could get hold of, and now maybe I would be able to break through the barrier. At last I might be able to understand this man and be permitted into his life.

I was right, but I had no idea of the price I would have to pay for my fascination fuelled by fear. I still ask myself sometimes, if I had known what was going to happen, would I have still done what I did?

All these years later, I can still say with conviction: 'Yes, yes, yes!'

## Chapter 3
## The Trap

At this stage in our relationship things happened all the time that I only fully understood months or even years later. I was young and trusting and I never looked further into things when perhaps I should have.

But, in retrospect, I realise my openness and innocence protected me. It was so new to Peter. Before we met he had become disillusioned with women, all of whom he saw as calculating, predatory and untrustworthy. This feeling had come firstly from a disastrous marriage to a calculating and promiscuous woman when he was in his early twenties, and then by the realisation that his stunning good looks, money and charm enabled him to bed almost any woman he wanted. He was sickened by what he saw as the shallow and fickle nature of women and he callously went out of his way, every time he was with a woman, to prove to himself that he was right.

He often did this by setting traps. Now he was waiting for the opportunity to set one for me, and I naively handed it to him.

Peter had invited me to London to see him and I explained to him that, as Alicia and Geoff were away for three months in South Africa, I wouldn't be able to stay with them as I usually did. To my surprise, he invited me to stay at his house – the first time he had ever done so. I was thrilled, believing that at last I was getting closer to him, and perhaps he would let me really love him. I was that naive!

We arranged to meet at six o'clock in the evening at the Carlton Towers, a hotel just a few minutes' walk from his home and one he used regularly. I decided to take a morning train so I could enjoy some window shopping and spend some time in London.

As I sat on the train a voice suddenly said, 'Well, hello – fancy seeing you after all this time!'

I looked up. There stood Jamie, one of a group of friends I had made while working as a model in Birmingham. There had been about ten of us and we had all mixed and partied together. Jamie and I had never been romantically involved, but we became very close friends, almost like brother and sister. Of all the people in the group, he was the one I could pour my heart out to about anything and everything, including my love life, and he did the same with me. Since there was never any sexual tension between us, our friendship had been genuine. But after I married André, Jamie and I drifted apart, only exchanging Christmas cards and the odd phone call. We hadn't seen each other for over two years.

'Can I join you?' he said, flopping into the seat opposite me without even waiting for my reply. 'Of course I can,' he added, laughing. 'You look wonderful, Helen. Tell me everything. What are you up to? How are the children? Are you happy?'

I hesitated for a second, but then I was back with my dear friend. The years vanished and we talked just as we always had. I told him all about my disastrous marriage, my divorce and the children, but when it came to Peter I was cautious. I said very little, only that I had met someone else and was on my way to London to see him.

'You're in love.'

'How do you know?'

'It's written all over your face but you're afraid to talk about it. Remember, I know you.'

I went very quiet and after a few moments I replied, 'That's true, Jamie, you do, better that many people.'

We chatted easily all the way to London. He told me of his happy marriage to another girl in the group, and I could tell from the way he spoke that he adored her. They had no children yet, but they were trying hard, he said with a grin. He had also been successful in business and was on his way to a meeting and dinner in London. By a strange coincidence, it was at the Carlton Towers.

I had already decided that, as I was not meeting Peter until early that evening, I would leave my suitcase at the hotel so I didn't have to carry it around the shops. It was natural that, as Jamie and I were going to the same place, we should share a cab.

When we arrived Jamie said, 'Hey, my meeting's not till three, let's have some lunch together' and it was just as natural for me to say yes. Of course, I was at that time unaware of Peter's cynicism about women; if I had known I would probably have been more hesitant about accepting Jamie's invitation. But I never once thought that my having lunch with an old friend could possibly pose a problem. I had hours to wait for Peter and, unexpectedly, I had a close friend to keep me company. I had no intention of hiding anything from Peter; in fact, I couldn't wait to tell him of my good fortune.

At that moment, the trap was set. Much later I was to discover that someone in the hotel had reported back to Peter that I had arrived, very animated, with a young man in tow and we had just gone into lunch.

The Rib Room at the Carlton Towers was very fashionable at that time and renowned for its freshly-carved roast beef. The smell assaulted us as we walked in. I had been there before with Peter and knew just how good it was. There were always lots of well-known faces in the restaurant and, when I was with Peter,

they often came up to say hello to him. Jamie and I
enjoyed recognising people as they came and went,
some of whom acknowledged me.

It was nearly three o'clock when we finally left,
Jamie to attend his meeting in another part of the
hotel and me to look around the shops.

I returned about five o'clock and sat down in the
lounge to wait for Peter. Six o'clock came and went:
still no sign of him. That was unusual, as he was
meticulous about punctuality. When he had still not
arrived by seven, I phoned his home, to be told rather
abruptly that he was not there.

I was starting to worry by now, and I was also
conscious that people were looking at me. Twice, men
actually approached and tried to pick me up, asking
me if I would like a drink or dinner. I felt very alone
and suddenly rather scared. What would I do if Peter
did not come? I had nowhere to spend the night and
very little money.

At ten o'clock I phoned his home again – he was
still not there. I sat down and began to think. With so
little money, where could a young woman safely spend
the night alone in London? I could sit at Euston
Station all night, but I didn't think that was very safe.
I wondered if they would give me a room at the Savoy
Hotel and charge it to my father's account. But even
if they did, I would have a lot of explaining to do to
my father – not so much about the money, but why I
had ended up in London, unescorted, late at night
without anywhere to stay.

Just then I remembered Jamie had told me he was
staying the night at the Carlton Towers. I sighed with
relief. If Peter didn't come, which now seemed very
likely, I would wait for Jamie and ask for his help.

At this time, I could not possibly know that I had
enemies – powerful enemies, people behind Peter who,
for all the right reasons, believed he couldn't afford to

have a close relationship; who believed he needed to stay single-minded, without any other pressures or loyalties, to be able to do his job successfully. It was in their interest, and that of the office they served, to do everything in their power to see me fall like all the women before me. They would go out of their way to make it happen, considered it their duty. Now I understand why and I believe they had nothing against me personally. They had a job to do and they did it superbly. But then I knew nothing of all this.

It was now well after eleven o'clock and, after I had been offered a drink by yet another man who was very persistent and didn't seem inclined to take no for an answer, it dawned on me that people thought I was on the make – available, or something even worse.

Just then a man approached me whose uniform indicated he was a member of the hotel staff . 'Madam, can I help you? Are you waiting for someone?' His tone verged on rudeness and, guessing what he was thinking, I retorted angrily, 'Yes – my husband.'

A look of disdain and disbelief spread across his face. 'I see, madam. Is he staying in the hotel?'

'Yes he is.'

All my life I'd acted impulsively and this was a typical example. I was quick to react to a slight, sometimes too quick, and I didn't give myself time to think beyond the immediate consequences. There were times when this was a very positive trait, but it could also be disastrous.

'Could you tell me his name please?'

'Mr James Cricklade,' I replied.

'Thank you!' He walked away, only to return five minutes later. 'I think, madam, it would look better if you waited in his room. As we were not expecting you, please would you sign in.'

He passed me a registration form. I assumed he thought I wouldn't be able to fill it in correctly and so would be unmasked and asked to leave the hotel forthwith. But of course, I remembered Jamie's address and telephone number, so I promptly filled out the form and signed 'Helen Cricklade' at the bottom. I handed it back to him, unable to resist a smile.

'Room 239, madam. Here is the key.' He walked away.

I considered my position. It was after eleven o'clock. Peter obviously wasn't coming, Jamie's dinner might go on very late and the hotel had made it perfectly clear they did not want me to wait in the lounge any longer.

I got up and walked to the lifts. The trap was now sprung.

When I reached Jamie's room, I was relieved to find it had twin beds separated by a table and a large chair. I settled into the armchair and began to reconsider my position. I wasn't worried about Jamie's reaction: we knew each other too well for there to be any misunderstanding. He knew I was not 'that kind of girl', and I knew that, once I explained, he would respect my position.

But now I began to have the first flutters of anxiety about what Peter might think. After all, it was fine to have lunch with a male friend, but how could I explain ending up in his bedroom? I tried to work out why I was worried. After all, Peter was an experienced man of the world. But, despite that, something instinctively told me he might not understand.

Of course, Peter already knew I was there, but I was blissfully unaware of this. From the moment he was informed of my arrival in the hotel with Jamie, he had set up a trap for me to fall into – and I had well and truly fallen.

Soon after midnight I heard a key in the door and Jamie came in. Just as I had hoped, he knew straight away that something was wrong.

'Helen – what is it? I knew as soon as they told me my wife was in my room that it was you. Are you all right?'

His kindness and understanding were so reassuring that I felt tears well up, but fought them back.

'Yes, yes, I'm okay, Jamie. My friend didn't turn up and the hotel thought I was some woman on the make, and I had nowhere to go so I bluffed I was with you.'

'Well so you are – so relax. That's what friends are for. There's the bathroom, there's your bed. I'll go down and get your luggage. Bastards, all of them,' he said.

When he came back with my bags I told him the whole story. Being a little older and wiser than me, the only comment he made was, 'I wonder if this has anything to do with you having lunch with me.'

I said nothing.

Jamie was very sensitive about the whole situation. 'I'll use the bathroom first and hop into bed, then you can take as long as you like. Tomorrow morning I've got to be gone by 7.30 anyway, so you can use the room until it's time to check out.'

When he came out of the bathroom he jumped into the far bed, turned away from me and said quietly, 'Good night, Helen. Sweet dreams.'

As soon as my own head hit the pillow I was asleep. I suppose that was surprising, in the circumstances, but then I knew I was safe and I was also very, very tired.

Next morning, I woke to an affectionate note from Jamie: '*Helen, order breakfast or anything else you want, it's on the company! Remember, we're friends and always there for each other. Good luck, whatever you decide to do, and keep in touch! Love, Jamie.*'

The fabulous thing about Jamie was that he listened and sympathised without trying to tell people what to do. That was why I had always valued his friendship so much. Often, when we try to help someone, we give unsolicited advice, or even try to take charge of a situation, which is usually the very last thing they need. But it is far more important for someone just to listen and understand. I was so grateful Jamie had done that. I didn't want anyone to tell me what to do. I knew I was in the hands of something stronger than myself and I needed to sort it out.

Of course at this point I had no idea just how much stronger. I had no idea of the forces ranged against me, and I'm glad I didn't.

What I did have was a burgeoning love for a man I was only just beginning to understand. I had begun to see through the coldness and sarcasm, into the person who had rescued me that night in Marbella when the spring had uncoiled and all his defences had come down.

I would have told Peter about the Carlton Towers fiasco anyway, but some instinct told me that it was vital he knew from me as soon as possible what had happened in the last twenty-four hours. So I decided to beard the lion in the den. I got up, dressed and, in case he was not at home, I wrote a letter to him outlining what had happened and why. By eight-thirty I was walking with my luggage to his house. If he was there, fine; if not I would catch a train home. But one thing I knew for sure – I was not going to leave London with him unaware of what had happened.

When I arrived at the house, the cleaner was sweeping the outside steps, the door stood open and, on another impulse, I walked straight in.

A man immediately confronted me. 'Can I help you?'

'Yes, would you please tell Mr Royce that Helen's here.'

I was afraid he was going to stop me so I quickly turned right into what I knew was a reception room.

He looked bemused and hurried off. I just had time to sit down and pick up a copy of The Times when I heard footsteps which I recognised as Peter's. He entered and looked at me without smiling. There was not even a glimmer of recognition in his eyes.

'You are either very brave or very stupid, or perhaps you are both.'

I said nothing, there seemed nothing to say.

'You will leave here in the next sixty seconds or you'll wish you had never been born.'

'Why – what have I done?'

'I won't even honour that remark with a reply.' He walked over to the door and held it open. 'Leave now before I do or say something I regret.' He looked at his watch. 'You have thirty seconds.'

I stood up. 'Peter, please listen to me. Please just give me ten minutes and then if you want, I'll go. I know you're a fair man. Please listen to me.'

His eyes narrowed, there was a long pause. 'You have ten minutes.' He walked over to a bookcase, leant with his back against it and crossed his arms. Then he proceeded to stare at me with a fixed, mask-like expression.

'I want to tell you about yesterday. I presume you're angry because I had lunch with Jamie. I want to tell you what else happened, but you'll probably be even more angry when I do. And I'm not brave. I'm quite frightened, and I'm not stupid. I need you to know about yesterday because I would never deceive you or lie to you.'

So I told him everything, from the moment Jamie had joined me on the train to his departure that morning. When I got to the part about going to his hotel room I thought Peter would react in some way, but he didn't, not a flicker. I urgently wanted him to; anything would have been better than that blank, frozen expression. When I had finished he just turned

33

away and appeared to be reading the titles of the books in the bookcase.

Oh, God, I thought, how can I reach him? Why does he push me away so hard? Then I remembered Marbella when he had walked along the beach with me, yards apart – keeping me at a distance. I remembered when we first met up again over a year later and he hadn't touched me for weeks. And I recalled the more recent times, when it was as if a light had suddenly gone out in him. How could I switch it back on?

Then it came to me – just be open and honest and risk telling him how you feel. I spoke quietly. 'I need you to believe me, Peter – that's how it was.'

He swung round. 'Why do you need me to believe you?'

'Because I love you, I want to be with you and I need you.'

It was the first time I had told him I loved him. It was so very true and although I was terrified of the confession, knowing I was leaving myself so vulnerable to him, I knew it was the right thing to do.

'I'll go now, my ten minutes are up.' I turned towards the door but as I reached it his hand came from nowhere and slammed it shut. I jumped.

'You are not going anywhere – sit down.'

I sat down. Although I was frightened, I was also relieved. The impersonal machine had disappeared. At least now Peter was here with me.

'Right,' he said, 'answer these questions.' And he began what I can only describe as an interrogation, firing questions at me with mind-boggling speed. The strange thing was, the questions were not about the facts; they were all about my motives.

'Why did you have lunch with him?'

'Why did you go to his room?'

'Did you consider any other options?'

'When you went to his room, what did you think would happen?'

'Why didn't you come here?'

'What did you think I would think about it, or were you hoping not to tell me?'

Finally he stopped. I almost felt dizzy, as if he had hit me.

I managed a weak smile. 'Can I answer those one at a time?' He said nothing, so I continued: 'I had lunch with Jamie because we've been close friends for years. We did all sorts of things together before we both got married.'

'Like what?'

'Oh, we'd go out together if either of us was short of a date. Four of us shared a flat in Birmingham, two boys, two girls. A group of us all went on a ski-ing holiday once.'

'I presume you've never shared the same bedroom before?' he said sarcastically.

I paused again, but only for a brief moment. 'Well, yes I have, actually. When we went ski-ing we stayed in a hostel and when we arrived we found we were in a dormitory for ten.'

Peter made no comment to that, then he said, 'What did you think when I didn't turn up?'

'I thought perhaps you were on a delayed flight from somewhere and would come directly from the airport, especially after I phoned here and they said you weren't here.'

'You never thought the reason might be something to do with your lunch date?'

'No – and it wasn't a date, it happened quite spontaneously. But later, in the room, Jamie suggested there might be a connection.'

'Why did you go to his room?'

'I felt it was the only safe option and the hotel staff were putting pressure on me.'

'But you lied to the hotel. Why?'

'Yes, I did, Peter. I didn't like them assuming I was trying to pick someone up when I wasn't. I wanted some credibility.'

'Why didn't you tell them you were waiting for me?'

'By this time I'd begun to realise you were definitely not coming. It was late and I was sure they would tell me to leave.'

'When you went to his room what did you think would happen?'

'Nothing – absolutely nothing. Jamie and I are good friends. He's very happily married to another friend and we trust each other completely.'

'What if he *had* got the wrong message and tried something?'

'I would have been astounded and very upset. We've never thought of each other in that way.'

'So how *do* you think of each other?'

'I told you, Peter, he's my friend – a very close friend, but there's no sexual attraction on either side. We just really enjoy each other's company.'

'How could a man enjoy a woman's company if he doesn't find her sexually desirable? I can't imagine that.'

I said nothing, but I registered this as something to think about later.

'How did you think I was going to feel about you sleeping with another man?'

I sighed. 'I didn't sleep *with* him, Peter, I slept in the same room as him.'

'Answer the question, Helen.'

'I thought you would trust me,' I said quietly.

'Why should I? I don't trust any woman.'

I said nothing, suddenly feeling this was a dangerous area to venture into.

36

The interrogation was not over yet. Peter demanded, 'Why didn't you come here?'

'There were lots of reasons. They told me you weren't here and I've never been to your house without you. I was afraid I'd miss you if you arrived at the hotel while I was gone. And when I suggested I could wait here, the man on the phone didn't sound very friendly.'

'But you came this morning – why, what was the difference?'

'Yes, I did. I decided I couldn't leave London without you knowing what happened so I wrote you a letter. I was going to drop it off on my way to the station. But when I arrived, the door was open and I came in on impulse. I felt that if I could get past your staff and you were here, it would be far better to tell you to your face than in a letter.'

'May I have the letter?'

'Yes of course.' I opened my bag and gave it to him. I had written quite simply:

*Dear Peter,*

*I'm sorry we missed each other yesterday. It was obviously one of those days when everything goes wrong – or it was for me anyway. I had lunch with a male friend who I met on the train and who was fortuitously staying at the Carlton Towers. When you didn't arrive I decided the safest option was to share his twin-bedded room. I know I don't have to justify that to you. I look forward to speaking to you soon. Love Helen.'*

He read it and re-read it, then left the room. I waited. How could someone not understand? I thought. There were many men whose company and conversation I enjoyed without thinking of them in a sexual way. Yet Peter had clearly never experienced a platonic relationship with a woman, and from what he said, he didn't want to.

Much, much later, I grew to understand Peter and

what had happened to him to make him think the way he did. But for now, I had to take a leap of faith, somehow sustaining my belief that this man was very special and would one day come to me as my friend.

The door opened. It was Peter, looking as if nothing had happened. 'Helen, let's go out to lunch – but I don't think we'll go to the Rib Room.' He was grinning.

I smiled back. 'No, I don't think we should either.'

Later, much later, after a wonderful lunch and a long, sensuous afternoon of lovemaking, Peter took me to Euston station to catch my train, even accompanying me onto the platform. It was almost as if he couldn't bear to leave me. As I was about to board the train he said, 'You know, Helen, I've never had a female friend in my life.'

'Well, you have now.'

'Have I? Who's that?'

'Me.'

He paused for a long time. 'That's an extraordinary thought,' he said finally.

'Do you have a problem with it?'

Another long silence, then: 'Yes, maybe I do – a big problem.'

He smiled and I waved goodbye. The train drew out and I was left with my thoughts. There were many things I still didn't understand but from that day, Peter decided to trust me as I trusted him. Thankfully we never had that kind of conversation again, and he set me no more traps.

## Chapter 4
## The Sword of Damocles

I looked at my watch. It was over two hours since Peter had left me, locking the door behind him. The room now felt cold and damp and I shivered. My reflections had led me to no conclusions, only to more questions that I desperately needed answered. Something told me they soon would be.

For now, there were more urgent demands: I needed the toilet and I was desperately thirsty. I felt panic rise in my throat.

The door opened and Peter walked in. He had changed out of his business suit into a pair of canvas slacks and a casual shirt, and was carrying a tracksuit which he threw into a corner of the room. Automatically I stood up, knocking the chair over in my agitation. My growing fear echoed in the brittle noise it made as it hit the floor. Peter took the other chair, turned it backwards and sat astride it.

'Sit in front of me and listen,' he commanded.

I picked up my chair and sat down. He paused and looked at me. I met his eyes. They were implacable.

'The next two hours will probably be the most critical of your entire life. At this moment you are in the Headquarters of the Intelligence Services. I am head of one of their departments and you have blown my cover.

'First, Helen, I must ask you again: have you told anyone else what you said to me in the car or shown anyone the photograph?'

'No, I haven't,' I said quietly.

'Speak up! Are you sure?'

'Yes, Peter, I'm sure. I didn't even tell Jessie, and I usually tell her everything.'

'Right. I'm going to tell you what you have got yourself into. Then I'm going to tell you what you have to do for it to be okay. Do you understand?'

I could only nod.

'I do not work for a travel agency. I am not a playboy. My name from birth was Edward Peter Harper, but I was always known as Peter, and my maternal grandparents were Royces. For the last fifteen years I have been Peter Royce. I work in Intelligence, running a highly secretive department that does not officially exist. It is sometimes referred to as "the Department that does not exist", though we just call it the Department. There are no records, no salaries, no employees and no contracts. We are totally deniable.

'You have now endangered that. You are a potential threat and any potential threat must be dealt with immediately. I have two choices: I can eliminate you or I can bring you inside. For the last two hours, I have been persuading my colleagues that you have what it takes to bring you inside. Now I have to prove it. So you will appreciate that the next sixty minutes or so are crucial.'

He paused. I could hear my breathing. It was ragged and uneven. My fear was so palpable, I could almost touch it, smell it. My heart was hammering so hard in my chest, I felt sure he could hear it. Yet, despite my predicament, my most pressing thought was how much I needed to go to the toilet.

'I'm sorry. Please could I use the toilet?' I said.

Peter raised an eyebrow. 'Yes, and change into this whilst you're there.' He got up and threw the tracksuit at me. I caught it. Then he opened the door and pointed at a room further down the corridor. A man sprang to attention and stood watching me closely as I hurried to the toilet and went inside. Once there, I took three or four deep breaths and tried desperately to control myself. I felt sick, wanted to cry, but I knew that both would be a mistake. I went to the toilet, washed my hands, looked in the mirror. My face was deathly pale, the eyes wide. I noticed that I was biting my lip. 'Come on,' I said to myself, then quickly took off my skirt and blouse and pulled on the tracksuit.

Back in the room, both chairs had been removed and Peter was standing against the far wall.

'Helen,' he said, 'you have to prove to the Department that you are suitable. You have to prove now that we can trust you.'

'How can I do that?' I said, my voice full of despair.

'You have to show that you will do whatever we ask of you. You must obey me without question, accept whatever I throw at you. You must not fight back and you must stay in control. Everything that happens can be seen and heard from behind that mirror.'

In my mind I went back to the night on the beach, to the moment when I realised I trusted him. 'You're fighting for my life, aren't you?' I said.

He didn't answer but for a split second his eyes gave him away. I became calm, the fear retreated. It was still there, but behind me somewhere, I sensed he was rooting for me, willing me to succeed ... I felt a transfer of strength and courage. As the calmness enveloped me, I knew exactly what to say. I was back on the beach in Spain and the words came out effortlessly: 'I will do whatever you say.'

There was a flicker of remembrance in his eyes and then silence. After what seemed a lifetime he said, 'From now on you will call me sir. Do you understand?'

'Yes, sir.'

'Then come here.' I walked towards him. As I approached he raised his right hand across his body and when I was close enough, he backslapped me hard across the face. I stumbled backwards, trying to keep on my feet, but I hit the wall behind me. Shocked, I turned into the wall and cradled my face in both hands.

'Turn around.' His voice was cold and quiet. The fear came at me head on and gripped me again. Until now, the only violence I had ever experienced was from André, and that had been hot, unbridled, often easy to avoid, and over as quickly as it had emerged. The violence I sensed in Peter now was passionless, calculated and disturbingly controlled. I was terrified.

'Turn around,' he insisted. Other words rang in my head. You must obey me. Stay in control. We have to trust you. Eliminate ... eliminate ... eliminate.

I turned, closing my eyes and putting my hands over my face.

'Put your hands down and look at me.'

Slowly my hands came down and I opened my eyes. His hand was raised again as if to hit me. I froze and waited. Suddenly he turned and walked across to the other side of the room, taking a packet of Benson and Hedges cigarettes and a lighter from his pocket. He stood there and nonchalantly lit one.

'Come here.'

I walked towards him.

'Take this.' He put the lighted cigarette in my right hand and, taking my left hand, he turned it over so the palm was facing downwards. 'Put the cigarette out on the back of you hand,' he said clearly.

I couldn't believe it. I looked first at the cigarette glowing in my right hand and then at my left hand. Finally I looked at Peter. There was no expression, no longer any acknowledgement of me in his eyes. I thought I might distinguish something, anything: sympathy, encouragement, even just an awareness of my gaze. But it was as if I did not exist, as if he was dealing with a machine. Yet this was the man with whom I had been intimate for the past nine months. I had begun to pride myself on getting through to him, at least a little. Unlike his other women, I had survived more than just a few weeks. I really thought that I had tentatively touched something in him that he had believed was dead.

Then I remembered: *'I'm a ruthless man, Helen, I use people. Sometimes they get hurt. Is that a risk you are willing to take?'*

I understood now how ruthless he was. He would do whatever was necessary, and nothing and no-one would get in his way, including any feelings he might have for me. Now I knew what I had to do. I was fighting for my survival and I was on my own. Yet I also knew that I believed in the same things as he did, so somehow I would make it.

I turned the cigarette so that I was holding it like a pencil and jabbed it fast and hard into the most fleshy part of my hand, between my thumb and index finger. I held it down, knowing I had to so that it would go out. The pain was intense. I twisted the cigarette hard as I had seen people do in an ashtray. Then it was over. It was out.

I was conscious of Peter still holding my left hand. Slowly, I handed him back the now extinguished cigarette as the pain began to subside. I tried to unclench my teeth but they seemed locked. I looked straight ahead at the wall. Peter dropped my hand and for the first time I became aware of the smell. Horrified, I realised it was the smell of burnt flesh. I backed away from him until I felt the wall behind me. Then I looked towards the door, seeking an escape.

His voice filled the room. 'Come here.'

Everything in me rebelled. I wanted to scream, 'Go away! Leave me alone!' but a little voice said 'No! No! Show them!'

'Come here,' Peter repeated. I noticed there was a

fresh cigarette alight in his hand. I walked towards him.

'Hold out your left hand,' he said.

I thrust it out in front of him, palm down, looking at him defiantly. Slowly, very slowly, he lowered the lighted cigarette towards my hand. I gritted my teeth and willed myself not to move. I didn't look down but continued to stare at him. He took my hand and slowly connected it to the burning tip. I felt sick. Sharp daggers darted in front of my eyes. I remember the pain as the heat burned into the same spot on my hand ... then nothing.

When I came round, I was on the floor. I felt sick and dizzy and the pain in my hand made me cry out. As things became clearer, I saw there were now two other men in the room, standing on either side of me. Peter stood in front of me but further away. He looked withdrawn, detached, almost bored by the whole situation.

'Get up.' His voice was icy. I managed to scramble to my feet, but immediately one of the two men pushed me back down. I tried again, but the other came at me. I kept trying, but each time one or the other forced me back onto the floor. All the time, I could hear Peter's voice, quiet but insistent.

'Get up, Helen.'

I don't know how long I kept trying, but eventually I succeeded in pulling away from the men. They followed me. I stumbled to the wall and tried to use that as my support, then I found the door and hung onto the handles, but they pulled me off. Eventually I sank to the floor again and lay there only half-conscious, tears pouring down my cheeks as Peter's voice continued like a stuck record: 'Get up. Get up. Get up'

Hauling myself to my feet, I clung to the wall. Everything stood still and I could feel myself swaying.

I tried to freeze. One man left and came back with a chair. The other almost peeled me off the wall and sat me on it. Then they left and there was silence.

I stood up. For a second Peter remained silent, removed, then suddenly his expression changed. First there was a flicker of an eyebrow, then his face relaxed and finally his mouth broke into a smile and the dimples I loved so much appeared on his cheeks. At that moment I wanted to cry so hard that it hurt, but something told me not to.

'Okay,' he said, 'everything is all right. Go and change, then come back here. I'll come back to you very shortly.'

'Yes, sir.'

He looked surprised. 'You can stop the "sir" now.'

Gingerly, I headed for the toilet. The two men were standing in the corridor. When I got there I splashed cold water on my face and let it run over my wrists. I looked at the back of my hand. A large black and purple patch had appeared and the skin was raw, blistering and red around the edge. I had nothing to soothe it so I just left it. I changed back into my skirt and blouse, pulling the sleeve carefully over my hand, which was now throbbing badly. Then I hung the tracksuit on a peg behind the door and returned to the other room.

I sat on the chair and waited, conscious that I was being watched. But I felt calmer now, the fear was receding again. My thoughts began to unjumble and, like a jigsaw, pieces slotted into place – slowly at first, quite precisely, then faster and more haphazardly until I became muddled again. There were too many pieces: some fitted perfectly but I was unable to look at those; others, I felt, might fit if I could just turn them round slightly, see them from a different angle. It was frustrating. I grappled with the pieces, trying to examine them, but I was tired and the more I tried the worse it became.

At that moment Peter walked back into the room with an older man who was carrying a bag.

'Helen, this man is a doctor. He will dress your hand.'

The man smiled, a warm, kindly smile, then he gently began to clean and dress my hand.

'As soon as that's done, we shall leave,' said Peter.

'Where are we going?' I heard myself say.

'Back to my house. I need to talk to you.'

## Chapter 5
## The Contract

The taxi moved very slowly, inching its way through the thick smog. Since deciding to leave the car in the car park and instructing the cabby where to take us, Peter had said nothing, but to me the lull was a relief, allowing me to collect my thoughts. I was incredibly tired; I was also excited, curious, puzzled. I wanted to know so many things. I wanted answers but I didn't dare ask the questions.

So, he was some kind of real-life James Bond, but with a sinister twist. I mean, the good guys weren't supposed to behave like this, were they? What I had experienced in the last few hours was bizarre in the extreme, so different from anything I had ever read or imagined, yet somehow I didn't feel all that shocked – just frightened. I was also fascinated.

I sneaked a glance at Peter. He appeared relaxed and at ease.

He caught my eye. 'Are you okay?' he said.

'Yes. Can I talk to you?'

'Later,' he said and took my right hand in his. It was warm and comfortable and I settled back into my thoughts.

How could he be so nonchalant and relaxed after what had just happened, what he had just done to me? Or was that all quite normal for him? Would he really have killed me, or had it just been a threat? Who were 'they'? Was I safe now?

He put his arm around me and drew my head into

his shoulder. As if he could read my thoughts, he said, 'Don't worry. It's going to be all right.'

This sudden gentleness threw me.

'I love you, Helen.'

I couldn't believe what I was hearing. In the last nine months I had come to believe I would never, ever hear those words from this man.

The taxi wasn't making much progress. Peter was gently stroking my arm and I was conscious of the raw masculine smell of him as I nestled into his body. My left hand was throbbing and I could feel the swelling inside my mouth where he had slapped me, and taste the blood as it seeped from the cut. What was I doing with this man who one hour ago was prepared to kill me and now said he loved me? Half of me wanted to jump out of the taxi and disappear into the London smog, the other half wanted him to make love to me.

The cabby grunted, 'We've got down to the bottom of the mall, sir. Do you want to walk from here?'

'Take us to Victoria Station and we'll walk from there.'

'OK, Gov'nor, it's your money.'

As the taxi drew to a halt Peter took out a large man's handkerchief folded it into a square and gently handed it to me.

'When we get out, Helen, hold this over your mouth and nose and breathe through it.'

The tenderness I had only glimpsed over the last nine months was now laid out before me like a cloak over a puddle. Something had changed and I didn't understand what it was. Why should you care about the smog? I thought. Why should you care if my bronchial tubes fill up? After all, an hour ago you were prepared to torture me, to kill me if necessary.

Now I was angry. I turned away as the taxi stopped and jumped out. Peter paid the cabby.

'Fine! You lead,' I said abruptly.

He raised an eyebrow but said nothing and we set off. We arrived at his house in one of London's loveliest squares. The Georgian portico greeted me through the smog. We walked up the steps through the doors and into the hall. The butler took my jacket. I asked if I could use the phone and made a quick call to check on the children, pleased that I managed to sound quite normal. We climbed the stairs into the drawing room on the first floor. The carriage clock on the mantelpiece chimed, telling me it was half past eight – over five hours since Peter had left me in that room, over seven since I had foolishly asked that question in the car. Or was it foolish? Perhaps not.

Wearily I sat down and looked around the beautiful room. A dark red Chesterfield dominated the wall opposite the panelled doubled entrance doors. The walls were covered with pale green, hand-blocked silk, the floor with an Aubusson carpet bordered by a highly polished oak floor. The sash windows were framed with burgundy velvet curtains, the tiebacks picking up the rich colours in the carpet. On the walls were several paintings, one I recognised as a Turner, and in one corner stood a Davidoff humidifier. It was a room that reeked of understated good taste. All it lacked was a touch of femininity. I wanted to put some flowers or a plant on the stern Georgian tables, perhaps soften the room with more indirect lighting and pretty ornaments.

Peter sat down opposite me. 'Are you angry?' he asked casually.

'A little.'

'Good. I'll get Paul to ring Alicia and Geoff and tell them you'll be staying with me tonight.'

He left the room. Luckily my suitcase was already here, as I was going to pick it up after I had brought his car back into London. At least, I thought, I have my overnight things and a change of clothes.

I got up and went over to one of the windows. The smog had closed right in. Even the streetlamps in the square had all but vanished. It was strangely quiet with no traffic. As I looked, the insipid light from a lamp picked out a spectral figure on the steps below. I barely discerned the outline of a man in a trilby hat and long coat as the door opened and someone let him in.

Peter came back into the room. He had put on a midnight blue smoking jacket with a silk cravat. Behind him was his butler Paul carrying a large silver tray with a bottle of champagne in an ice-bucket, the ice cubes rattling as he walked. On the tray there were also two tall crystal champagne flutes, two large plates of smoked salmon and some brown bread and butter. As the plates were placed on the table I realised I was famished; I hadn't eaten all day.

Peter was grinning . He looked young, boyish, utterly carefree. 'Geoff said they'll see you the next time you're up in town,' he said.

'Oh – was that all?' I felt slightly deflated. But what more did I expect? Of course to Geoff it would all seem quite natural that I had decided to stay with Peter. With the smog and the inevitable cancellation of Peter's flight, he wouldn't suspect anything.

'Yes, that's all,' Peter said, handing me a plate of smoked salmon. 'Eat.' He passed me the cutlery and the brown bread.

'Thank you.' I sat down and did as I was told. It did flutter through my mind that I would like to throw the plate at him but it was only a feeble flutter that my brain dismissed almost immediately. Although I was ravenous, I felt slightly sick so I ate cautiously at first. Then my taste buds were stimulated by my favourite food and I wolfed it down.

Looking up, I surprised Peter in an unguarded moment and caught a fleeting glimpse of tenderness and warmth in his face, which disappeared instantly when he saw me looking. He handed me a glass of champagne.

'Now drink this, but not so fast.'

I giggled. I think everything was beginning to catch up on me and I felt slightly hysterical. I tried to stop it but the giggle escaped and ran out of control.

Peter got up, walked behind me and placed his hands on my shoulders. 'Steady, steady. Take some deep breaths. There are some people you have to meet in a minute. Then, Helen, you will know who "they" are.'

Oh God! I thought. It was the men behind the mirror, the men who, with Peter, had held my life in their hands, and still did.

Peter went over to the fireplace and tugged at a long tasselled cord. The door opened and Paul ushered in two men, both in their late fifties or early sixties. One was fairly short with podgy features and, oddly, he was wearing a pair of white gloves. The other was tall, distinguished and confident-looking.

Peter walked towards them. 'Sir Max, Sir John, may I introduce you – this is Helen.' He didn't tell me their surnames.

The men shook my hand. They seemed charming, especially the tall one, Sir John. The other man, the one with the gloves, appeared rather shy and self-conscious. Yet as I smiled at them, I could not forget that, for all their charm, only a short while ago they had been demanding my death. I understood even then that together they were a formidable pair.

In an almost surreal scenario, they welcomed me to the Department. They told me I was part of the most elite section of the Intelligence Services, congratulated me and then left. I never saw Sir John again but I met Sir Max a few times over the next years and he always wore gloves. I learned eventually that it was because he suffered from the skin disease psoriasis and was deeply self-conscious about it. It also left him desperately shy.

After Sir John and Sir Max had gone, Peter lit the fire. I watched the paper catch the sticks and the flames ignite and begin to leap in intricate patterns. He turned down the lights and sat on the Chesterfield, a brandy goblet in one hand and a cigar from the humidifier in the other. His legs were gracefully crossed, the firelight caught his features. He looked so very much the urbane Englishman – a picture of sartorial elegance.

Peter began to talk to me. As he did so I sensed a feeling of relief settle over him, as if he was sailing into a harbour after a storm, or coming home to a place where he could be himself. As he talked, the chiselled contours of his face softened and the boyishness I had perceived earlier heightened.

He explained that a contract would now be formed between us – no more lies, ever. If he couldn't tell me the absolute truth of a given situation, he would say so. The same would apply to me. If I was confused, misunderstood things, got them wrong, I had to tell him. That way, he said, I would be in no danger. As trust built up between us, I would learn more. Eventually he hoped I would become more deeply involved in the work of the Department.

'I admire your courage, Helen, and you have a fine brain – you think very fast and have a great ability to collate and retain information. We need that and we can use it.'

Things were changing so quickly. I felt exhilarated.

'You will now be living in two different worlds and you will have to be able to separate them,' he explained. 'I believe you can do that. When you are in the one outside the Department, you will have to be an actor on a stage. You must become someone else – someone who has not seen what you have seen today

– and live and believe in that person. But at the same time you must never lose a grasp of this new reality – you will have to live with how things are and what we in the Department actually do. That is something you share with me and no-one else.

'The other thing you share with me and no-one else,' he continued, 'is my real identity. That is the most dangerous information you will ever be party to. There are only two other people in the world who have that knowledge and you have just met them.'

'May I still talk to Jessie?' I heard myself say. 'I'll never disclose who you are.'

'Yes,' he said.

I was surprised but incredibly relieved. It was so important that I should be able to talk to Jessie, have someone to confide in.

'Some of the things we do you will not like, but they are necessary. I accept that you will not like them but don't think you can comment on or discuss such matters. You'll get short shrift from me. Decisions are made, not from emotions, but from an absolute conviction that those are the right decisions required to protect this country.

'We are not Gods, Helen, but someone has to do what we do. We live with our decisions and anyone suspected of becoming arrogant or having an ulterior motive is dealt with. There are no compromises or excuses. Retribution is immediate and merciless. If people bring their own personal agenda into decisions, they are eliminated.'

The detachment with which he spoke both terrified and enthralled me. He told me that there were three things in this world that caused most of the problems: money, sex and power. Money was not an issue for members of the Department, as they all had private wealth. As for sex, the unequivocal rule of the Department was that members must avoid all emotional involvement.

He looked at me and paused. 'So you see, Helen, I cannot afford to care.'

It was as if he had hit me again. A large piece of the jigsaw fell into place. Now I understood the coldness, the cruelty, the continual distancing.

'I was in trouble this afternoon, Helen. It was a close-run thing. I had to agree to kill you myself if necessary.'

I felt a cold shiver run up the back of my neck. 'Would you really have done that?' I asked quietly.

'Yes.' His eyes looked at me directly.

He was right, there was no compromise. They were merciless.

Power, he told me, was probably the most dangerous of the three. It creeps up on people insidiously and from behind, and they are often unaware of its effects until it is too late. Very few people can handle it once they find it in their hands. But it is the most seductive of mistresses.

'In the Department, we have to watch for it before it takes hold, and stamp on it very hard. No one is excused. Again, when you see this happen you won't like it but you will say nothing. Do you understand?'

'Yes, I think so. But Peter, can we go back one step?'

He nodded curtly.

I spoke carefully, feeling my way for the right words. 'This afternoon I know you said that you had to persuade your colleagues about me. How did you do that?'

'I had to convince them of two things: one, that if it came to making a choice, I would put the Department before you. Two, that you in your own right were someone of value to us. Both those things, Helen, are reality. Make sure you never forget that.'

'But ... but ...' I almost whispered, 'what about your feelings for me?'

'My feelings for you are of no importance.'

'But you don't deny them?'

'No.'

The eyes were still implacable. I shook my head. How could he be like this? How could he possibly say these things? I had never before experienced such devastating honesty. I had always been taught to wrap things up if they were sensitive or hurtful, but now I had to accept a completely new value system.

Part of me welcomed it. I remembered in Spain the night Peter told me straight that André was an alcoholic. I had really needed someone at that time in my life to cut through the fudge, not to paper over the cracks, to present me with reality. Maybe another part of me didn't much like it but at least I knew where I stood with Peter. It confirmed the belief and trust I had in him, and now I realised why he commanded such respect from those around him.

'Helen, I told you a few minutes ago you will get the truth from me or I will not answer your questions. But remember, if you ask questions the truth can hurt.'

'Do you love me?' I heard myself say before I could stop the words.

'Yes.'

I shook my head again, unable to reconcile myself to my situation. Even now, as I write this over thirty years later, I find it frightening. That day, in just a few hours my whole life changed. Suddenly it took on another dimension. Suddenly I was part of something that had worldwide significance. Suddenly the naive girl became a knowing woman.

It must have been after midnight before he stopped talking. Then he took me there in the beautiful drawing room in front of the fire. When he made love to me, it was different from any other time. He released a torrent of feeling that I had never imagined belonged to him. When I opened my eyes, the flames lit up his face and

I saw again, deep in his eyes, the warmth that was so new to me.

That night was the first night he ever let me stay with him, and that night I learned why.

At some point we went to his bedroom and fell asleep entangled together. Two or three hours later I was awakened by Peter writhing about on the bed. He was having a nightmare. I tried to wake him as he lashed out and cried: 'No – no!'

I sat up and tried again but his flailing arms hit out at me. 'It's coming – it's coming!'

Then he was awake. He turned onto his back and the light from the hall illuminated his features. I saw that he was staring at the ceiling. I couldn't believe it. This was the man who was so strong, so controlled. Tentatively, I put out my hand. He was sweating, yet also cold and shivering.

'Darling,' I said.

He didn't answer. I moved across and into his space. His arms closed around me and he held me very tight, so tight I had to gasp for breath.

'Darling – I love you,' I said.

He held me tighter and gradually the shivering passed.

'They all died,' he said.

I said nothing. Something told me this was a pain way outside my experience, a pain that would never go away. I held Peter close as his breathing gradually evened and he went back to sleep.

This nightmare tormented Peter for the rest of his life. I never did find out the story behind it, but I suspect that, for security reasons, he had been forced to make a decision that resulted in the deaths of innocent people. The guilt was crucifying him, and it never stopped. Eventually it took its toll on his health and, I am convinced, contributed to his untimely death.

# Chapter 6
## Isolation

The following morning, after I had left Peter, I experienced for the first time a feeling that would beset me for the rest of my life: a feeling of loneliness and isolation that is hard to describe.

I was heading home to Cheshire. When I arrived at Euston Station, there was still an hour to kill before my train left so I decided to have a coffee. Sitting in the buffet I looked around me and started to people-watch, something I had always enjoyed. Yet now it felt very strange. It was as if I was watching a movie, or in the middle of a bad dream, or looking through the wrong end of a telescope. I gripped the table in front of me and blinked hard, but the feeling wouldn't go away. The only thing that still seemed real was me. I wanted to shout out loud to the people surrounding me: 'Stop! Wake up! What are you doing? Don't you see?'

No, of course they didn't and why should they? I was hugging a great secret that they didn't know. All of a sudden I had a heightened sense of perception. To me, not understanding, everything and everyone seemed so shallow, so complacent and inane. How could they just rush around like ants? Didn't they ever stop to think what life was all about? All around me I saw men and women with the average 2.4 children, the twenty-five-year mortgage, the nine-to-five job. They worked, slept, ate, watched TV, went to the pub, partied with friends, made love, quarrelled, made up, took two weeks holiday, went back to work.

They struggled to pay the bills, bring up the kids, better themselves – then what?

Of course it wasn't them – it was me. I was the one who was out of step. I was the one who was now different, no longer a member of that club. When an egg has been broken you cannot put it back into the shell – so what do you do with it? You discard it or make it into something else. Peter had certainly broken the egg, and he could so easily have discarded it. But he had fought to allow it to be made into something else. I was the raw ingredient waiting to be used in his recipe.

I rubbed my eyes. What was the matter with me? Maybe I was just overtired. Would I ever again be able to just sit down with people and enjoy idle chit-chat about everyday things? I felt so isolated.

Did part of me, at that moment, regret losing a more ordinary, mundane existence? Yes – and part of me still does, some thirty years later. From that day, a vital element of my personality had to be stifled. If it had died it would have been easier, but it was still inside me, demanding to be heard and hurting because it was being suppressed. And it is still there today.

Ever since that first morning, I have struggled with moments of depression when I have felt far removed from normal people and everyday life. It is a desperately lonely place to be. It rarely hits me when I'm on my own. Nearly always it is when I'm in a crowded place, watching other people, or part of a group. I suddenly feel out of things, a spectator rather than a participant, desperately wanting to say all sorts of things that I cannot say, unable to share my real thoughts or the real me. Some people pick up on this and wonder if it is because I'm shy. Others believe that I hold back because I feel superior.

Of course, neither is true. It is just that I know and have seen things that I cannot share, and for me sharing has always been a vital part of my life. I believe that confiding one's experiences and feelings to another person enriches both parties and is the only way to be truly intimate, and I had, until that day, always enjoyed being open. Now that intimacy and openness had been denied me. Renouncing them was a huge sacrifice, but for Peter I would have done almost anything.

I had to sacrifice my natural gift for forging close friendships, and it hurt so much. Thank goodness, then, that I still had one friend I was allowed to confide in, as long as I protected Peter's identity: Jessie, the very person who had indirectly – and unwittingly – disclosed that identity. Jessie, my wisest, dearest friend. How lucky that was.

That morning at Euston was my first experience of just how different my life was going to be from then on. The world I had entered didn't exist for other people, and in entering it I had lost most of the realities that do exist for others. People whose reality and perceptions are different from the norm, and who do talk about them, are sometimes labelled insane. Yet, as a result of my own situation, I now wonder if some of them are not perfectly lucid. Perhaps what they are saying is true, but incredible or unacceptable to so-called 'normal' people. After all, 'normal' people crucified a man who said he was the Son of God.

As for me, I couldn't talk about the reality of the world I had entered, so people could not judge me on that. They could only judge me on what they saw, and they saw a woman withdrawn into herself. While new acquaintances saw me as shy or reserved, old friends, I believe, were hurt. They sensed a distancing in me, an unfathomable change. Some thought it was the divorce. Not many pursued it, though a few were more persistent and would ask me questions – Geoff and Alicia in particular, who really noticed the change in me. They knew I was seeing Peter, and sometimes we all went out together. But what I couldn't share with them was who he really was, what he really did, what had happened.

One night Geoff said to me, 'A lot of people, Helen, think they're close to you and know you well, but I suspect they don't. I thought Alicia and I were very close to you but in recent months you seem to have put up a glass shield and very few people, if any, get behind it. I don't believe we now know the real you at all, and I find that sad. I wonder if anyone does, and if so, do they know how to take care of you?'

I heard the friendship and love in his voice and I felt my isolation more keenly than ever, and a deep sadness.

'Perhaps I don't know myself,' I replied flippantly, but of course I did.

Geoff just shook his head.

Over the next few months we drifted apart. I had to distance myself from him and Alicia and they felt it. In sacrificing my friendship with them, I hurt us all.

Peter alone understood the position I was in, because it was one he knew all too well. He had his own unique way of dealing with it. He purposely immersed himself in the company of people who could be perceived as leading inconsequential lives, people who often appeared to have no other purpose in life except to enjoy themselves. Then he became one of them. They ranged from film stars, actors, racing drivers, gamblers, socialites, the aristocracy, minor royalty, the bored, rich and famous – worst of all, the hangers-on.

I learned, thank goodness, that not all of them were by any means as shallow as they appeared. Some were playing a game, some the same game as Peter. They pretended to be totally hedonistic, but were actually working for the Department. These people led lives that appeared to be an undemanding round of parties, gossip and fun, and in such a world others never got too close. No-one asked too many questions because they saw no depth. Everything was superficial. It was the perfect cover.

Peter's cover was brilliant. He moved in this circle and acted the playboy role to perfection. It was like a complete metamorphosis. As a result, people underestimated him. Their defences came down and they would reveal information that could be of vital interest to him. When I realised this, another major piece of the jigsaw slotted into place. Until then I had been puzzled by the places Peter took me to and the people we met when we went out. For instance, we sometimes went to the nightclub Annabel's and to me, still innocent of Peter's identity, many of the people there had seemed fatuous and bored, consumed with the need to be seen in all the right places and with all the right people. I had tried in vain to work out what Peter saw in them. Now I understood.

His lifestyle reminded me of Sir Percy Blakeney's in *The Scarlet Pimpernel*, and I told him so. He was amused and we often laughed about it.

Slowly I began to realise how precious it was for Peter to be able to relax and be himself with someone, especially a woman. The distance he had kept, his shunning of intimacy, made absolute sense to me now, all the more because at that time I began to do the same thing. It would be over ten years before I found anyone else who I allowed anywhere near the real me. When I did it was the ultimate gift because, after Peter's death, I had accepted that it could never happen again. That man eventually became my husband and I am still with him today. Like Peter, he is unique, and it was Peter who led me to him.

But more of that later.

I learned to dissemble, to play a part. I grew adept at hiding most of my feelings from everyone and I became a chameleon as circumstances demanded. Though I tried to learn how to handle the loneliness this caused, I didn't succeed.

Only with Peter was I real. Only with him did I share my deepest self, and of course this made us closer than ever, and me more dependent.

I became obsessed with him. I was consumed by him, addicted to him. He was the sun, the centre of a solar system he had created and I was the nearest star in his constellation. This somehow reminds me of the belief some North American Indian tribes have that if you save a person's life, then that life becomes yours. Peter had saved my life; it became his and I revelled in it. This could have been a totally negative thing, an assimilation of one individual by another. But it wasn't because despite or maybe because of the world he lived in, Peter had fallen in love with me.

Part of that love manifested itself in a coaxing out and nurturing of dormant strengths in me that I was completely unaware of. Peter had a magical gift of demanding and getting the very best and more out of people around him. And because he loved me he pushed me even harder that anyone else. He said I could do something, so I did it. He told me I was good at something, so I was. For the first time in my life someone really believed in me and my confidence soared. It was heady stuff.

When I was away from him I just lived for the moment I would see him again. I met this man when he was reaching the very peak of both his masculinity and his brilliance and, like a surfer, I rode on the crest of his wave. He had come back on the scene just as I reached a crucial crossroads in my life.

I had married very young, met Peter when I was only twenty-three, had two children by the age of twenty-four. My upbringing had groomed me for nothing more than being an upper-class lady who sat at home arranging flowers and doing good works from the comfort of her *escritoire* – but that was not me at all. Except for the pleasure my children brought me, I was lonely and unfulfilled. And even though they were central to my life, I needed intellectual and emotional stimulation at an adult level which my situation at that time denied me.

So when Peter came back into my life, he was like a bright comet from outer space.

Neil, one of the men who was always with him, once asked me if I'd had a previous career. Had anything prepared me, he wondered, for the moment when I suddenly found myself right next to Peter?

I thought about it. Jessie always said I had inherited my father's intelligence and my mother's mercurial quick thinking. I had grown up very close to my father, who had taught me to read and encouraged me to talk to him seriously from a very young age. He had awakened and nurtured my love of literature and music, discussed serious subjects with me, instilling in me a natural ease with powerful intellectual men like himself. Boarding school from the age of seven had then imbued me with a certain stoicism: one had to cope. It had also given me the finest education money could buy, but so far I had done nothing with it.

All this had lain dormant when fortuitously I had landed in the hands of a master. The personal training Peter gave his top people was of the highest order; it didn't come any higher. It was the most exacting learning experience I could have gained anywhere, and it began immediately.

## Chapter 7
## Jessie

So now I was back in Cheshire. It was at this point that my friendship with Jessie, which had always been important to me, became vital. Peter must have been aware that I was going to need a confidant and he had quickly determined that Jessie was the right person to fill that role.

Born shortly after the turn of the century, Jessie was brought up in a strict Methodist upper-class family. During the Second World War she had been a senior Red Cross nurse and travelled extensively through India, Burma and Malaya, ending up in Singapore, where she organised the repatriation of British prisoners of war from the Japanese camps. Brave and resourceful, a typical English memsahib, she had experienced war with all its horrors. She had never married, but during this time she had enjoyed a few close relationships with senior officers away from their families. Two of these were famous Allied Commanders, known throughout the world.

It was typical of Jessie that she never told anyone except me. One night we sat together reading all the letters and studying the photographs that had passed between her and her lovers, before she ceremoniously put all of them on the fire. She was determined there would be no evidence after her death to support rumours that might detract from these men's lives and hurt innocent people. As the letters and photographs shrivelled on the fire, she cried softly at the memories they evoked. I cried in sympathy. It was a special moment between us.

Jessie had known me since I was born, but I only really remember her from when I was about ten, when she was already in her fifties. Her parents and my grandparents had been very close friends, and in her twenties she had nearly married a close relative of mine, only turning him down because he was younger than her. He remained the love of her life and that is why she had never married. She said I was very like him in looks and character, and we hit it off immediately. The forty years between us were invisible, the generation gap no more than a tiny chink: we were kindred spirits with the same passion for life and zany sense of humour, natural friends who understood each other perfectly.

As I progressed through adolescence to adulthood, Jessie was the person I could always talk to. She never criticised me or told me what to do, but would sometimes gently chide me and suggest other options. Over the years her influence on me was immense. It was Jessie who looked after the children when my parents couldn't, Jessie whom I entrusted with those things most precious to me. When I came back from Spain after my first meeting with Peter, it was to Jessie that I poured out what had happened and how I felt. It was Jessie who warned me to be careful when I started seeing Peter again, and it was to the haven of her house that I fled when I got back from London that day.

And now it was Jessie whom I trusted with this information. I told her what had happened. I told her what Peter really did, what I was now involved in. All I did not tell her was how I had broken his cover or who he really was.

She wasn't shocked. I don't think she was even that surprised because she already suspected that Peter was more than he'd told me. Having been close to powerful leaders herself, when I had talked about him she had recognised the type.

In her sixties by this time, Jessie had seen so much of life and she was wise and discreet. She loved me and, even more importantly, she understood me. Though she was worried, she did what she had always done: she was there for me, listened to me, supported me, and that was what I needed. From that moment she became my sole confidante, someone who made no judgements of me, just offered unconditional love and advice.

She never realised she had been investigated by the Department but I knew she had, otherwise I would not have been allowed to talk to her. The only caveat from Peter was that I must never tell her about the photograph or his real identity. I think she may have guessed but she never asked and we never spoke of it.

Jessie continued to be an indomitable spirit way into her nineties: a dear friend and one of life's beautiful people.

# Chapter 8
# Betrayal

It was a typical English summer day and I thought we were going to a party. Peter had told me to meet him at Manchester Airport at ten in the morning and to bring a change of clothes. 'Dress down,' had been the instruction, which I found a bit strange.

The air was clear and the countryside basked in sunlight. I didn't know where we were going and I didn't really care. But after I picked Peter up I became conscious that he was driving *into* Manchester, not out, as I was expecting.

'Where are we going?' I asked him.

'This is business, Helen – it's official. I want you on parade now.'

'Yes, sir.'

That was the way we worked: 'on parade' or 'off parade'. 'On parade' meant obeying a set of rules, military in their precision and exigence. They had been drilled into me by Neil, one of Peter's ADCs, until they were almost engraved on my brain.

'Understand, Helen,' Neil had said, 'you are either "on parade" or "off parade". When "on parade" you follow these rules.'

He repeated them, then repeated them again. I questioned him to make quite sure that I understood them.

'And when I'm "off parade"?' I asked.

'Then, Helen, I can't advise you. I suppose you follow his personal rules.' A wry smile crossed his face.

'And what are those?' I asked.

He looked at me kindly. 'I think you already know.'

I often wondered what Neil felt about the situation between the man he called 'the Boss' and me, but I never asked. I knew how loyal he was to Peter. I remembered him from Spain, he had rarely left Peter's side.

It was some years later that I found out what he thought.

So I understood the rules. Heaven forbid that any of us should try to break them, but then I never wanted to. I was proud to be involved, to be one of the elite. Nothing could have induced me to do anything that might jeopardise my place. I'd already had to fight long and hard to gain some kind of acceptance by Peter's professional entourage – all men, much older than me, all brilliant in their own fields. But they were beginning to accept me and I intended to stay there and become part of the Department. I wanted to be one of them.

We arrived outside Strangeways Prison, a grim and foreboding place, and walked through the front gate. Peter waved some form and a man escorted us along endless corridors with white walls, stone floors and small windows looking out onto courtyards where prisoners walked aimlessly around the perimeters. Everything seemed still and lifeless, the eerie calm interrupted only by the scraping of keys in oil-less locks and the opening and closing of doors as we went through.

To me, the prison warders seemed to be jailed by the rigidity of the system just as securely as the inmates were by the cell doors that clanged shut behind them. I was not impressed with this system and could see no point to it, except to keep dangerous men or women off the streets and away from the public. Otherwise, the jail appeared to be the perfect training establishment for the criminal, and a dehumanising place for everyone else associated with it. I decided that day that the prison lived up to its name: Strangeways indeed!

We seemed to go deeper and deeper inside. Sensing the prisoners' restless pacing all around me, I was glad I had put on a nondescript skirt and top and had covered my blonde hair with a headscarf. 'Dress down,' Peter had said and now I knew why.

As we walked he spoke to me in a quiet, clipped tone. 'You are about to see what happens when someone betrays us. You will not like it. I don't expect you to. But you will witness it and you will say and do nothing. Do you understand?'

'Yes, sir.' I looked at him. In his coldness he seemed unreal, as if inhabited by something more machine than human.

We stopped at the end of a corridor outside a door. The man unlocked the door and stood aside as we walked in. It slammed shut behind us and the keys scraped in the lock, then the sound of footsteps faded as he walked away.

I heard an intake of breath and looked around. On the far side of the room, which measured some ten feet by ten, stood a man – medium height, stockily built, early thirties. He was clean-shaven with sandy hair and his face bore an expression that was a curious mixture of fear and aggression. Peter signalled me to stay behind him by the door as he slowly approached the man.

When he spoke it was so quiet I could hardly discern what he was saying, but the tone was like a shaft of ice pitched across the room towards its target.

'You knew I'd come, didn't you? Oh yes, you knew I'd come. This is for Graham and the others.'

Peter's movements reminded me of a brilliant swordsman's, except his only weapons were his hands.

Karate chops landed fast and furiously as the man
tried to raise his fists but he was far too slow. He
seemed to disintegrate in front of my eyes. Within
seconds blood was spurting from his nose and he was
screaming. The sound sickened me and I retreated into
a corner by the door, realising that I was trapped in
this horror.

Yet still I watched. I didn't want to but something
held me and I didn't dare turn away.

Peter then systematically beat the man to a pulp.
That was what I found so terrifying. The beating was
shocking enough, but even worse was the control and
efficiency with which he did it. The precision of the
whole thing reminded me of someone pruning a rose
bush, making quite sure that each cut was delivered
to exactly the right place, so that the end result would
be perfect: the complete physical, mental and
emotional destruction of another human being.

There was no anger in Peter's actions, no passion
at all. It was cold and relentless. I wondered if he was
going to kill the man and I realised that I hadn't the
slightest chance of stopping him. Here was someone
who didn't make mistakes and I knew with chilling
certainty that I was in the presence of an expert.

By now blood stained the walls and the smell of
urine and worse pervaded the room. A noise I had
never heard before emanated from the man. Mixed
with the sound of the blows it was like a pop song
from hell. Every time the man hit the floor, Peter
dragged him to his feet. I tried to cry out 'Stop!' but
my voice wouldn't work and all that came out was a
squeak.

This seemed to make matters worse as Peter heard
me. After a quick glance at me he dragged the man to
his feet and threw him across the room in my direction.
I jumped out of the way as his body hit the wall next

to me and he slumped to the floor. I could hear him gasping for breath.

I ran across the room to the opposite wall, passing Peter going in the other direction towards the man. It was like some menacing caricature of a children's playground game. He ignored me, ignored my fear. It was as if I wasn't there.

When he reached the man, Peter picked him up, turned around and threw him again directly at me. This time I anticipated the move but I still did not move fast enough. As his head thumped the wall alongside me, blood and gore spattered me.

As that point I started to heave. Then, just as I thought I would lose control, Peter stopped. He stopped as abruptly and completely as he had started. It was as if the man lying on the floor had never existed, and nothing had happened in that room at all.

Walking to the door, Peter banged on it three times. It opened as if by magic and he beckoned me to go ahead of him. I stumbled into the comparatively fresh air of the corridor, gagging for breath, desperately trying to stop the retching in my stomach.

Peter stood there with the prison official, or whoever he was, waiting for me to pull myself together. 'Take some deep breaths.'

'Yes, sir.'

I was acutely conscious that there was no sound from inside the cell. Was the man dead? As I regained control of my stomach, other questions spun into my mind. Who was that person? What had he done to 'betray us', as Peter had claimed?

I looked at Peter. He looked utterly unfazed, uninvolved, not even breathless as he talked rapidly to the other man. I was stunned. My mind was unable or unwilling to consider what I had seen. I just wanted to escape the fetid stench of fear in that cruel, inhuman place.

At that moment I was more afraid of Peter than I could have ever believed possible. I wanted to remove myself from this man, as quickly and as far away as possible but I knew that was not going to happen. Unless he released me from "on parade", I was locked in this hell. I knew for certain that if he'd touched me then I would have screamed and screamed and been unable to stop. I was in shock but I did not know it.

We walked down the corridors, through the front gates to the car, which was right outside. The sunlight streamed down but I felt no pleasure in it.

Peter jumped into the car, tore off his filthy white T-shirt and flung it onto the floor. Reaching onto the back seat, he grabbed a clean one and put it on. The whole action felt to me like the discarding of something lower than low, totally worthless – a thrusting aside of every aspect of the man he felt such contempt for. It shocked me almost as much as everything else that had happened. The way he did it was like another act of violence.

Grabbing a box of Kleenex from under the dashboard, Peter pulled down the sun visor and checked his face and hair in the mirror. Handing me the box he told me to do the same. 'You can change in a minute,' he said.

I stared down at myself. Now I knew why he had told me to bring a change of clothes.

We drove out of Manchester in silence. I couldn't think of one thing to say and I was still trying to control my physical reactions. Looking down at my skirt, amongst the smears of blood and other bodily fluids were solid bits of what I realised were human flesh. I was horrified and started to shake. Peter's reaction was to lean across into the glove compartment and pull out a bottle of something. 'Drink,' he said, and I did. The liquid was cold and very sweet.

We reached the hotel outside Manchester where

Peter was staying. He got out of the car, signalling me to do the same, and told me I was 'off parade'.

When we were in the room I asked him if I could have a bath before I changed. He nodded.

On automatic, I went into the bathroom and quietly closed the door before running a bath. At first the warm water was comforting and with relief I sank down into it, but I couldn't get rid of the horrific images running around like demented ants in my head. I stood up, drew the curtain and turned on the shower as high as it would go, allowing it to beat into my body. It felt much better than the bath – more cleansing. Perhaps I could wash all the images away.

Then the door opened and Peter came in. He was naked. He came up behind me in the shower, enclosing my body with his. The water beat down on us. I was trapped, frightened. I knew what he wanted, I could feel it. He wanted sex and he was going to have it. Part of me submitted – the part of me that for some reason felt a need to pay for what I'd witnessed and my inability to stop it.

He was rough and threw me on to the bed, still wet from the shower. As I hit the mattress an unbelievable anger welled up from somewhere deep inside me. It was overwhelming in its intensity and immune to the thought of any consequences. I became a mass of kicking legs, scratching nails and biting teeth. I realise now how lucky I was that, faced with this little tiger cat, Peter chose not to retaliate. Instead, a devilish grin spread across his face and with the same deadly efficiency with which he had dealt with the man in the cell, he quickly subdued me and held me down.

After that it all became jumbled in my head, but if the act felt like rape, it felt right – because maybe that was what I deserved. I didn't know. I only knew that sometime later I was left sobbing quietly on the bed, feeling calmer.

Looking back, I can see that Peter knew exactly what he was doing from the moment we left that cell. He was making sure that the penalty meted out to traitors was indelibly imprinted on my mind. He had warned me from the outset of the Department's severity in such matters and then, at what I suspect was the first opportunity, he had seized the chance to hammer it home in the most disquieting way.

Now Peter had gone out for a walk and I knew he would not come back for several hours. I did not know then the personal price he was paying for what he had done that day. He was going through his own hell, and only years later did I understand that. For the moment, I had to live with the belief that the man I loved could operate, when necessary, like a robot, without the slightest trace of humanity towards anyone.

So what had the man in the cell done?

He had, I discovered, betrayed the Department and caused the deaths of three men, one of them an SAS officer.

Who was he and was he dead?

I think I know who he was but I don't know if he was dead. He might just as well have been, as I never heard his name mentioned again. He probably deserved what happened to him, because he had betrayed the country and people he had committed himself to serve. But the brutality of the retribution still disturbed me.

To this day the inner conflict I felt then remains: it is with how traitors are punished, not why. Other people may judge differently.

Whatever the case, this was the beginning of my real initiation into the Department.

## Chapter 9
## The Scarlet Pimpernel

I slept and when I woke up the first thing I was aware of was that darkness was falling. I turned onto my back and saw Peter sitting in the armchair under the window, watching me. When he saw I was awake he smiled.

'Hi! Are you feeling better?'

I couldn't help it, I was immediately overcome by the attraction of the man – the warmth of his voice, the dimples on his handsome features, the love shining from his eyes.

'What are you doing?' I heard myself saying.

'Waiting for you to wake up, Sleeping Beauty!'

I stared at him. He got up and came over to the bed, kissing me gently.

'What time is it?' I asked. 'How long have you been sitting there?'

'It's nearly nine o'clock. I've reserved a table in the restaurant.' He picked up the phone. 'This is room thirty. I have booked a table and ordered a meal in the restaurant. We'll be along in thirty minutes. Thank you.' He turned towards me.

'How long have you been sitting there?' I asked.

'A couple of hours.'

'What were you doing?'

'Watching you.'

I turned away. He didn't seem to mind and went back and sat on the chair, first drawing the curtains. I felt calm and, thank goodness, I no longer felt sick – in fact I suddenly felt weak with hunger, as I hadn't eaten all day. Being involved in Peter's world meant there were many occasions when all the normal routines like day and night, eating and sleeping, receded into oblivion as if they had never existed, only to re-emerge in a desperate bid to re-capture reality.

I was very quiet for a time, and so was he. Finally I said, 'I'm not sure I can tackle dinner.'

'Yes you can. Put some clothes on.' His voice was gentle, not demanding, yet it compelled obedience.

I got out of bed, went into the bathroom and dressed in my clean clothes. As soon as I was ready he took my arm.

'Let's go.'

In the restaurant, Peter told a waiter our room number and we were ushered to the best table in the place.

'Shall I bring your order now, sir?' said the waiter.

'Yes.'

We waited. I looked around the room, basking in its luxury. Peter said nothing. I didn't want to talk and I was aware he realised that. We sat in comfortable silence until the waiters arrived with the meal he had ordered. They bustled around with their silver service and soon a mouth-watering array of food was spread in front of us: sole veronique, creamed potatoes and minted peas. It was light and with a little encouragement I took a few mouthfuls.

Then I blocked. Peter cajoled me but I continued to block. I couldn't eat. There were too many images flashing across my brain, and they were too powerful. He accepted it without questioning me.

Eventually the waiters took away our barely-touched plates.

'You haven't eaten anything,' I said to Peter.

'I'm not hungry.'

I stared at him. After a long silence – a long, long silence – I relaxed back in my chair.

'Talk to me,' I said quietly. 'Tell me something about yourself.'

'What do you want to know?'

That was typical. 'Everything – anything ...' I said gently.

He started to talk – very slowly at first, gradually gaining momentum. I'm sure that he had never talked about himself to anyone before and it didn't come easily.

'I don't remember my parents. They died in an accident. I was brought up by my grandparents. At seven I went away to boarding school.' He hesitated.

'Were you living in England?' I prompted.

'Yes. There was a lot of money. I was an only child in a household of adults and servants. At thirteen I won a scholarship to Winchester, where I flourished academically. My grandparents died before I finished school. I was left a fortune but it meant nothing to me.'

I listened. From Winchester he had gone to Oxford, where he gained a double first in English and History. After that he grew bored.

'Everything had come too easily for me,' he said. 'I went into the RAF for a short period. There was a disastrous marriage for an even shorter one. After the divorce I found myself in my late twenties: wealthy, single, bored, disillusioned and directionless.'

I was surprised at even this slight bit of information. Although I had known Peter now for over two years, and it was a few months since I had broken his cover, this was the first time he had ever told me anything about his past.

He continued: 'It was at this point that "they" picked me up.'

'Who were "they"? I asked quietly, gingerly feeling my way.

He raised one eyebrow and looked up at the ceiling on the far side of the room.

'The main one was the then Prime Minister, Winston Churchill. He had just come back into power and he asked me to research the possibility of forming some kind of inner unit within the Intelligence Services, using some of the resources from the redundant SOE.* He wanted it to be impervious to infiltration, or betrayal by the likes of Burgess and Maclean; to be guaranteed free of any contamination from the main Security Services, which he believed still had moles and traitors within their ranks. It was therefore to operate with entirely new people, headed by myself.

'It was an avant garde idea and I was exhilarated. Churchill's enthusiasm infected me and I went away determined to find a way to make it happen for the great man.'

And so Peter had researched the whole thing for six months and gone back to the Prime Minister with his ideas. His key recommendation was the creation of a Department that didn't appear to exist, and he told Churchill how it could be done. The PM was passionate and totally committed, immediately authorising the setting-up of the Department and giving Peter everything he needed and more to get it up and running.

'And at that point, Helen,' Peter smiled, 'my whole life came together, its purpose, direction and meaning, and I have never looked back. I was able to bring the Department into being as I wanted, and in my own way.

'Churchill was a colossus of a man and people still do not know the full extent of his contribution to his country. He allowed radical ideas, totally new thinking and a realignment of power which even in a young man would have been brilliant. In him it was utterly remarkable. You have to remember that by this time

(* Special Operations Executive)

he was in his mid-seventies, yet his thinking was still far ahead of that of anyone in the country.'

As Peter talked, I noticed that his features were alight and the admiration he felt for Churchill shone from his eyes. This was a side of him I hadn't glimpsed before. To see Peter openly admiring someone else was something new.

'Were you very close to him?' I asked.

'Yes, I suppose I was.' There was a very long pause. 'He was probably the first and last person I ever came close to – until now.'

He took my hand across the table and his eyes swam with love. I felt a tremendous tenderness for him which was a new emotion. Perhaps it was aroused by the sadness I sensed in him. I had never seen it before and at that moment I felt very close to him.

We talked way into the night and he opened up more, letting me see inside himself. He recounted things he had seen and done in connection with the Department, places he had been to, people he had met, and how Winston Churchill himself had made the connections and introductions for him. It was a remarkable story and I hope all of it will come out one day.

But my story is concerned with the man who was the Department, rather than the Department itself.

I was privileged that night to be so trusted, to be allowed inside his heart. Peter told me of the loneliness of his childhood and how it had made him single-minded, first in his studies (hence the double first), then in his RAF career. He became a loner who formed no strong male bonds and after his marriage, his attitude towards women, although outwardly charming, became inwardly disdainful.

Somewhere in the early hours of the morning we fell asleep. When I woke up I realised again that my life had been changed forever.

After that day Peter involved me more in the work of the Department. He started taking me to meetings. At first I would sit quietly and listen but as the weeks passed into months, gradually he began to ask my opinion and I started to contribute. I met politicians, heads of state, heads of other intelligence services, even royalty. I learned quickly and knew almost instinctively when to fade into the background or withdraw.

The more I was with Peter the more my respect and admiration for him grew, on both a personal and professional level. He had so many gifts – intellect, moral and physical toughness, immense energy, single-minded devotion to his work, a creative imagination and the ability to inspire deep respect and loyalty. His love of his country was absolute. He was a master in his field. He succeeded in building up his authority and power to an astonishing degree through the confidence his personality inspired, and the willingness of others to delegate to him the responsibility of solving problems they could not or would not solve themselves. He refused to compromise, or accept anything from himself or any member of his team that wasn't the very best, and he never asked anyone to do something he would not do himself. He had no interest in any sort of personal popularity – in fact his own needs were completely overshadowed when he was working.

To me, there seemed no limit to what he could achieve.

But there were times when he was with me that I would see the absolute exhaustion on his face and understand the high price he was paying for his patriotism. Yet if I sometimes wondered what toll Peter's work was taking on his health, I always concluded: well, did it matter? What he was doing was so important. Maybe I should have worried more, realised that perhaps he was giving too much. But even if I had voiced such worries to Peter, I know he would not have taken any notice. He was far too committed.

The contrasts in our relationship when we were 'on parade' and 'off parade' were mind-boggling, but I was beginning to handle them better. The lows I sometimes felt were more than compensated for by the highs, when I knew for sure that this was what life was really about.

Peter still went away, of course, sometimes for weeks on end. Then I had to guard against those feelings of isolation when I mixed with other people – and the inevitable feelings of jealousy. One time I saw a photograph of him in New York coming out of a well-known restaurant with a famous and stunningly beautiful woman. I had to fight the demons inside my head that asked too many questions, for that was something I'd learned never to do with Peter. Anyway, I knew him well enough by this time to realise I had nothing to fear: if he was committed to the Department, it was clear now that he was also committed to me. I understood that to retain his cover it was essential he was seen with the beautiful people, and was considered to be one of them.

Sometimes he did things that were wild, spontaneous and thrilling. One day, for instance, I met him at Heathrow and he told me we were going out for lunch. Then he took me to a quiet part of the airport where a private Lear jet sat waiting on the tarmac. We got in and he took over the controls from the pilot.

'I didn't know you could fly a plane!' I exclaimed as we took off.

'You never asked.'

'Where are we going?'

'To Paris!' he said, grinning broadly.

'What for?'

'I told you, we're going out for lunch!'

Now it was my turn to smile. 'Who does the plane belong to?'

'Me.' He sounded very light-hearted and it was catching.

As we crossed over the coast Peter pointed out various landmarks and I heard myself singing 'When we flew over the white cliffs of Dover...!'

On reaching Paris, he handed the controls over to his crew, who proceeded to circle the city while we had lunch in the sumptuous sitting area, with the Eiffel Tower, Notre Dame and the Sacre Coeur beneath us. Peter sat back and began to hum the tune 'I love Paris'.

It was an idyllic day, one of the few when he was loving and gentle, making me feel as if I was the most important thing in his world. But I knew deep down that wasn't so: I could never compete with the Department.

Another time, before he took me on a Mediterranean cruise, he insisted I had some new dresses for the trip and one day handed me a sealed envelope. As I began to protest, he threatened to put me 'on parade' if I did. Later, when I opened the envelope, I found a large sum of money inside, more than I could ever need even for forty dresses. I took it and bought some beautiful clothes, then returned at least half of it to Peter in another sealed envelope.

'What's this?' he said.

'Your change.'

He threw his head back and burst into laughter. 'Helen ... you never cease to amaze me!'

'Why?' I said, puzzled.

'Well, this is a first!' He continued to chuckle as I grinned back at him.

'There's always a first for everything!'

Actually, I was very short of money. I certainly had very little to spend on glamorous clothes but I didn't want Peter to know that.

It was a strange situation. On the surface no-one would have known I was in difficulty. I had a house, a car, my parents made sure the children had all the necessities, plus a trust fund for their education. My mother gave me fruit and vegetables from their garden and eggs from the farm, but I was too proud to ask them for the cash that would have allowed me to live independently. There was no maintenance from André: drinking had consumed his life and left him with no money for anything else.

It never entered my head that if Peter had known he had a son, I could have asked him for maintenance. It was just something I would never have done. Anyway, I didn't want him to know. Although he seemed totally disinterested in my children I was worried that if he did find out, he might want some kind of stake in my son, even take him away from me. Peter's way of life and what I wanted for my children were in conflict, so I kept the two totally separate.

I had savings, but I had already begun to eat into them, so I found myself a job. It was only part-time, but it helped to keep our heads above water.

I remember once comparing a night out with Peter at the Ecu de France in London with buying the children and myself fish and chips as a Saturday night treat. They were worlds apart, but at least it was my own money that bought the treat and that was important to me.

I wanted to be independent, but it was very difficult. All the time I was with Peter I was dependent on others. Although I was grateful for the help I received, I wanted to be in control of my own life, yet it seemed that my father controlled one half and Peter controlled the other. This made me more determined not to have to ask anyone for money, and the little things I was able to do for myself – including giving Peter back his change – became very important to me.

When Peter was in one of his light moods, he was completely different. Away from his responsibilities in London he became carefree, amusing; almost childlike in the delight he took in my pleasure as he presented me with surprises. Once he had let go of his icy control, the simplest things pleased him.

I also discovered in him an immense knowledge and love of music and the written word. He would sit for hours with me, sharing an intensely beautiful piece of music. I would listen to him recite a piece of Shakespeare, and then we would discuss it enthusiastically together. He could quote poetry and passages from some of the world's greatest writers.

These were the best times, but there were too few of them. In the hours when I was hurting because of his indifference or even an attack on our love, I would cling to those times, playing the records, reading the books he had given me. I would hang in there and wait until he softened again.

Part of the training Peter had opted to do was a course at a drama school, which had taught him how to use both his voice and his body to maximum effect. He'd learned how to walk, how to make an entrance, how to make the most of his natural elegance and presence. Unsurprisingly, whilst there he had made friends with some of the well-known actors and actresses of his day. What surprised me more was when he told me that his advice had been sought by a film crew on how to play the role of James Bond in the early Bond films. Like most other people, I had always thought Sean Connery was so convincing in that part; now I knew why. Peter, with his natural sartorial British elegance and clinical coldness, was the ideal role model. Connery perfected his style, although I never did find out whether Peter coached him personally.

There has been much speculation as to who Ian

Fleming, the author of the Bond books, based the character of James Bond on. I believe it was probably a melange of people, including Fleming himself, as he had been in British Intelligence. He almost certainly knew Peter, and it was very obvious to me that, in the film, the character, background and style of Bond had a lot of Peter in it. Like Bond, he had lost his parents in an accident. He was the product of a top English Public School. He smoked, drank vodka and Dom Perignon champagne. He was always immaculate and elegant, and undeniably good-looking in a hard, masculine way. He had all the charm and breeding of his class. He was a man whom women noticed and men were wary of.

Of course Peter was not an operator like 007. His position was more like that of 'M', but even that didn't quite fit.

Whatever the truth was, during my time with Peter, everything became larger than life, and there was something almost novelistic about it.

I was immensely proud that he loved me. I understood what a great gift I had been given in being permitted to know this man so well. We never pledged permanency. Our love happened, and that was enough for both of us.

He summed it up so succinctly in a poem he once gave me:

> *'I can't be your mind*
> *nor do I want you to be mine.*
> *In loving each other*
> *We must stand apart*
> *And yet be one*
> *Using understanding*
> *As the force that will*
> *Keep us separated,*
> *And yet,*
> *Forever together.'*

# Chapter 10
# Training

Now my real training began.
If I thought that my life in the Department so far had been tough, then I was mistaken. As time progressed, I questioned how I felt, and I realised that for the first time in my life I was completely alive. At the end of the day, I would fall into bed exhausted but fulfilled in a way I had never imagined possible. I couldn't wait for the next day to begin and when I woke up I would jump out of bed fully energised and hit the ground running.

It wasn't that I was unaware of the dangers of my position. Peter had made them patently clear. It was just that I was so excited, so conscious that I was moving in an entirely new sphere, involved in something really worthwhile.

And of course, I was in love.

Peter wasn't the only one who needed something to fulfil his life. The difference between us was that I hadn't been looking for anything. Even though I knew, somewhere in my subconscious, that I needed more than the very real fulfilment my children brought me, I had pushed the thought aside and carried on as before.

But now I couldn't. After Peter came back into my life, it dawned on me how intellectually bored I was. He made me realise that.

Peter explained that he personally would be in charge of my training, most of which would be on the job. He warned me from the outset that, because I was a woman, it was going to be exceptionally hard for me to be accepted. The men at the top would reject me as long and as hard as they could. Not only would they be against me because I was a woman (this was long before the days of Stella Rimmington or Political Correctness), they would also be against me because I was 'the Boss's'. No favours were going to be shown to me; in fact, I soon discovered it was to be quite the reverse. Peter made it clear that, in his reviews of my progress, he would have to judge me harder than he would the men. He would not be able to help me gain acceptance; I would have to do that for myself.

I had never seen another woman in the Department. It consisted only of men. Of course, there were women in the conventional Security Services and women who worked for us without realising it – but there was none 'in the know', none at all. I was on my own.

I weighed up in my mind what this would mean, and determined quite quickly that I could turn it to my advantage. After all, my father had always told me that women were just as sharp and clever as men, and had innate skills that were perhaps even superior to men's in some respects. He had proved this belief by hiring a woman as the most senior Director in his company, which was very unusual for his generation.

My father had given me confidence with men and if I was honest, I actually preferred male company – though not for the obvious reasons! I just felt at ease with men. I was also not intimidated by men with power because, again due to my father, I was used to power. I loved watching it at work and, if at all possible, nudging and influencing it from behind.

For me, power plus patriotism was the absolute aphrodisiac.

I was ripe for what was happening to me, as if my whole life previously had been a preparation leading up to this. It seems trite to talk of destiny, but that's what I believed at that moment and that was the key to my enthusiasm.

The training was quite different from what I had expected. I suppose I thought there would be guns and gadgets, close quarter combat, Rosa Kleb with her steel toe-probe, bugging, shadowing people – all the things I had seen in the James Bond films. I thought it was all a question of 'Have gun, will travel.' But it wasn't.

Peter taught me that the finest weapon in a person's armoury is their brain.

'Learn to sharpen your brain,' he told me, 'hone it and focus it fully onto the problems that face you. Above all, learn to use the brains of the people around you.'

To be able to do that, to perform at our most effective, he drummed into all of us the fundamental principle of the Department: learn to know and control yourself first. He would always do this in the aftermath of complex operations when things had gone wrong simply because we were not in control of ourselves.

'Which is master within us, our logic or our feelings?' he would ask.

Eventually, after stumbling around searching for the answer, we would say 'our feelings'.

'So how do you control your feelings? Simply by getting in touch with them and learning to handle and control them, not by repressing, denying or avoiding them. If you repress and deny them, then you lose touch with your humanity and conscience. You become a psychopath, capable of justifying any decision by any logic, be it instigating the holocaust or removing an enemy because you do not like him.

'When operating, we have to close down our feelings so that our actions and reactions are based on fact and reality, unfettered by emotion. But, in the aftermath, we must then release our feelings. We must learn to live with and accept the fallout from them, however painful that may be. Only then can we keep ourselves balanced and sane and not turn into Daleks.'

I knew that Peter certainly kept in touch with his feelings. I had witnessed the nightmares.

'Power is one of the greatest problems we have to learn to handle,' Peter always said. 'In the Department we have checks and balances, so that no-one has absolute power. Absolute power corrupts absolutely, no matter who you are. The boundaries of power in the Department are defined very clearly and are rigorously enforced. Everyone takes his lead from the leaders. If the leaders permit corruption, evil and weakness, then everyone else in his team has permission to practise and preach it – and they will.'

Peter trained us in his own particular brand of practical psychology. We learned to get deep into our minds and into the minds of our enemies so that we could handle ourselves as well as them.

One of his favourite quotes was from the great Chinese leader, Sun Tsu: 'Know yourself – know your enemy.' If you could be certain what the opposition was going to do, then you could undermine their control whilst strengthening your own.

One morning Peter asked me a question. 'Helen, if there were two rooms, one containing physical pain, the other mental pain, and you had to go into one of them, which one would it be?'

I chose the mental pain. How naive that was!

Peter looked at me solemnly. 'Think back to when you broke my cover, to the time of the cigarettes and the burning of your hand. What happened when the pain became too intense? You passed out.'

I nodded, remembering.

'What is the most painful thing that has ever happened to you?'

'The mental cruelty at my first boarding school,' I replied.

'Yes. The burns on your hand are now just scars but the mental cruelty you suffered then will hurt you all your life.'

It was true.

'Handling physical pain is comparatively easy,' he continued. 'When it becomes too intense, you black out. The body can only take so much; it has its own safety net. But mental pain – that's something different. The mind can take a lot of stress and pain but when it does get too much, the safety net is more drastic. Pushed too far, the mind retreats into breakdown or madness. We must learn to release and handle our feelings to make them flexible and resilient.'

The pressures in the Department at Peter's level were almost all mental. Life-or-death decisions had to be made, sometimes at breakneck speed. On some occasions you would have too much information, making it difficult to clear away the fudge and attain the clarity of thinking required. On others there would be such a sparsity of intelligence that it was almost impossible to get any picture at all. This could result in having to make a decision using guesswork to fill in the gaps.

Then there was time. Time was always a pressure: too short, and one could be panicked into a decision. Too long, and one could find oneself going over the facts again and again, until what had once seemed transparent became convoluted and obscure.

I learned that time itself cannot be controlled, only its use. A decision had to be made at the right moment; that was as much a part of its importance as the decision itself.

I had to learn to be patient. We knew that we

needed to wait for the right moment or the right situation to arise before a decision could be implemented. Sometimes the temptation to move too early for fear of missing the boat was very powerful, but we had to learn to make that judgement.

For me, it was a major revelation that timing could be so important.

As for decision-making, I had always been taught, both at home and at school, that you should make a decision and then stick to it. This is bred into the British psyche through the military and public school system. Now I had to unlearn it, and fast.

In the Department, I discovered that all avenues must first be explored, then all feasible options must be kept wide open and a final decision made only when absolutely necessary. The result of this was that the maximum number of choices were kept available for as long as possible, and the opposition kept in the dark as to one's intentions until the last possible moment.

So, in the Department, one had to have control over one's emotions, control over timing and the patience of Job.

Peter explained that moral factors nearly always appeared somewhere in the equation, and had to be weighed against security factors. The safety of the state could depend on winning and keeping the moral high ground.

Then there was the matter of controlling the pressure, learning to take whatever came at us. Dynamic inactivity could be breathtakingly effective but it required immense courage and willpower. Peter showed me how people instinctively want to fight back if attacked, or to run away. This is called the fight/flight syndrome.

In the Department, giving in to the urge to fight, which was the instinctive reaction of most men, could be a grave misjudgement. Vital energy would be expended, rational thinking would close down and the anger invoked in responding to the provocation would result in a loss of self-control.

Peter taught me how to go with the flow, to wait for what was coming, whether verbal abuse or mental or physical pressure; to conserve energy and emotion whilst working out what to do. By staying in control, you hold all the cards even when appearing not to.

Developing this patience was particularly difficult for highly-trained, specialised military personnel. Many a hot-blooded SAS man failed to get into the Department because he had been so well tuned to respond fast and efficiently to attack. Asking them to sit back and wait was anathema to everything they had been trained for and their aggression was too well practised to sublimate or control. They had rapier-like reactions which were perfect in their own environment, but the very strengths that made them experts in their field worked against them in ours.

For us it could spell disaster.

It was also vitally important that we understood, and had under control, psychological pressure. When used correctly, it was a powerful weapon. The name of the game was to get into the enemy's mind, to understand what he was thinking and then exploit that to the full.

On so many occasions I saw the opposition destroy themselves while we looked on but actually did very little. Sometimes all we needed to do was generate fear, like the lion hidden in the undergrowth that lets out a threatening roar.

A public example of this was the Balcombe Street siege in London. As soon as the possibility of SAS involvement was voiced on the television, the terrorists gave up. The regiment's reputation instilled such fear and applied such psychological pressure that nothing else was necessary. I don't think 'the boys' ever had to leave Hereford!

Once you allow fear or panic to reign, you have the potential for loss of control. Once you have loss of control, you have sown the seeds of failure.

Peter taught me that by fanning that lack of control in others but holding onto your own, you would win. The psychology and training of the Department was based on this absolute belief: know and control yourself. Inside the Department lack of control would not be tolerated. Outside it was used as one of our strongest weapons.

And so another piece of the jigsaw slotted into place. Now I understood what had happened in that room after I had blown Peter's cover. It was all to do with control. Peter hadn't actually done a lot to me. He made me do it to myself, by manipulating my own self-control.

The selection procedure for everyone was based on the same principle.

At this time, there was one lesson I learned that I have never forgotten, and never will.

I was in a safe house outside Manchester, and Peter and I were sitting together in front of a large log fire. I was relaxed and happy, completely unaware that I was about to undergo a training session. But then this element of surprise was all part of the training.

'I want to talk to you about trust,' said Peter. 'The inner team of the Department relies on trust and it is something we can never take for granted. We have to instill it, and test it constantly. If there has to be honour amongst thieves, then there certainly has to be honour amongst us.

'If we lie, cheat, deceive or betray internally, the Department would never hold together. We would destroy ourselves. Our business is dealing with deceit, but we always have to be careful to keep it out of the Department. Anyone who becomes corrupted in the outside world and brings it into the Department is a traitor in every sense of the word. They must be dealt with ruthlessly.'

I thought of the man in Strangeways.

Peter continued: 'Trust in another person must be continually renewed. It is relative. It depends on many things. What are we trusting them about, to what degree? How are we trusting them, with what, about what, and relative to what?

'For instance – a man may trust his son, but not to drive his car. Lord Nelson could be trusted with the British Navy, but not with another man's wife.' He looked at me. 'Tell me, do you trust anyone, Helen?'

'Yes.' I looked straight into his eyes and said directly, 'You – I trust you with my life.'

'Then you are a fool!' he snapped. 'If I had to choose between the security of this country and saving your neck, what decision do you think I would make? Trust is one value where you have to weigh up your judgement each time.'

'No – I don't think so,' I retorted, without thought. 'Why shouldn't I trust you that way? Anyway, I do.'

'Don't challenge me, Helen.' He turned and left the room.

I sat there. You stupid girl, I thought. You stupid, stupid girl! Why had I pushed him? What was I trying to do? Did I really need to try and prove that he loved me more than the Department? Why couldn't I keep my mouth shut and enjoy things the way they were?

Damn it. There was this part of me that wouldn't let things go. I had always been the same. When I was a child my mother used to say to me, 'Why don't you drop it? You're like a dog with a bone.'

She was right, but even though I knew it was foolish, I still did it. Something inside me wouldn't be contained. It usually happened so fast that I couldn't believe where the words had come from.

This time, if I wasn't very careful, it would get me into serious trouble.

When Peter came back I was sitting in the same chair, staring into the fire.

'I'm sorry,' I said quickly.

He nodded. 'Don't ever trust anyone completely. Do you understand? Not me. Not yourself. No-one.'

'Yes – well, I understand that I can't trust myself.'

'Go on.'

'I can't trust myself not to do what I just did a few moments ago.'

'You're right! Part of you loves flirting with danger.'

'Is that what I was doing?'

'Yes.'

I was surprised. His interpretation of my behaviour was very different from my own understanding. Was he right? Had I been flirting with danger? Did I enjoy it and if so, why?

As if he read my thoughts he said, 'Do you know why you do it?'

'No.'

'Think about it – think about it right now. Why do you flirt with danger?'

There was a long pause. He was completely relaxed, as if he had all the time in the world.

'Fear excites me,' I said, 'it makes me feel alive, all my senses are heightened. Pushing through it is exhilarating ...' I hesitated.

Peter stood up and suddenly a gun appeared in his hand.

'What's the matter?' he almost whispered when he saw my face. 'Are you afraid now?'

'Yes.'

'How else do you feel?'

'Terrified.'

'You shouldn't have tested me.'

He cocked the gun. I heard the distinct sound of a round entering the chamber.

'Are you excited by fear now, Helen?'

'No.'

'Don't move!' he commanded. I sat there frozen.

I watched him steady the gun and aim it at me with both hands. I saw his finger tighten on the trigger. I closed my eyes very tight. Then I felt a sharp pain. Within seconds I was dizzy. That was the last thing I remembered.

When I opened my eyes, I was lying on the sofa. I felt weak and dizzy. The room wouldn't stay in place, everything was lurching backwards and forwards, then descending on top of me. I tried to back away and a half-scream came from somewhere.

As things gradually settled down I looked around. I was alone. As I concentrated the clock on the mantelpiece came into focus and I saw that over two hours had passed. Gingerly I inspected my body. There was no blood and no wounds. I was obviously not dead or even seriously injured. But my upper arm hurt and, on close inspection, I found a bruise there, surrounding a small puncture hole.

I felt exhausted. I lay back and closed my eyes.

I woke again to feel Peter's eyes on me. This time I felt almost normal. Then the fear came back. I said nothing, just waited.

When he saw he had my full attention, he spoke.

'Fear is a very powerful weapon. Perhaps the most powerful of all. You enjoy playing with a dangerous toy that you don't yet fully understand. You are like a child playing with a hand grenade – don't play with that weapon and don't play with me.'

That was probably the most important lesson I ever learned from Peter: to respect fear. If I was still tempted to play with it, Peter had now made me aware of how dangerous that was. He always drove home so hard the lessons that really mattered. What I had to do now was try and control that weakness.

Every lesson I learned from him, I learned by experience. It is, I believe, the only way you ever really learn. The lessons were hard and impossible to forget.

I had learned about the reality of violence from the incident in the cell in Strangeways. If I hadn't seen it, smelled it, heard it, I might still have thought it was all neat and tidy, as in a James Bond film.

Peter knew that it was impossible to control the world around us; but he also believed that if we had control over ourselves, as W E Henley said, we would be the masters of our fate, the captains of our souls.

That is what he was striving for personally all the time and that is what he was trying to imbue in us. One could not always control events, but one could control one's reaction to those events, whatever they were.

This was one of the most remarkable things about Peter and it made him stand out from other men.

It was about this time that I began to realise that this control also applied to the way Peter felt about me. He was absolutely determined to be in control of his feelings for me, and determined that they should never come ahead of the Department.

Although intellectually I accepted this, in my heart I didn't. I wanted to talk to him about it. I didn't want this rule to apply to him and me but I realised it was non-negotiable. I felt that if I did put pressure on him, he would eventually destroy me – perhaps physically, but definitely emotionally.

Yet I knew I couldn't stop myself. Gradually I was coming round to the conclusion that in the long-term we were doomed.

I was wrong, though I didn't understand it at that point. I do now

Control doesn't have to equate to being cold. People think being in control means suppressing your feelings, perhaps not even having them – it doesn't. It is the reverse. Control is being able to release your feelings when appropriate, then handling the feelings you have released. If you inhibit them you don't know them. You must know them to control them – otherwise they will control you.

I now understand the tightly coiled spring in Peter that I had seen for the first time that night on the beach in Spain. He was a man of high passions. He could release those feelings to their outer limits and still control them. This is what made him so incredibly broad, so unpredictable, so dynamic – such a challenge for me.

He was controlled fire, not ice, as most people perceived. This is what made him so exciting.

# Chapter 11
# The Swimming Party

Problems could present themselves at any moment, anywhere. You had to be prepared to deal with them whatever the circumstances, to drop whatever you were doing and take absolute control of yourself.

To begin with, I watched fascinated. Peter and his team could assume that control and slip from one world to another in seconds.

The first time I experienced this was at a party I attended in a safe house near Oulton Park racetrack in Cheshire. It was owned by a textile millionaire in Manchester, and was a beautiful place which lent itself particularly well to summer parties.

It was lunchtime and the swimming pool was surrounded by racing drivers and their ladies (whether wives or mistresses, I didn't know), various television personalities, film stars and wealthy local businessmen. Plagued by my usual feelings of isolation, I had moved away from the group, intending to go and see if Peter, who had been called inside to the telephone, was coming back out.

Without any warning, Peter appeared at the door. He called for me and four or five others, then led us quickly into a windowless room. Someone closed the door behind us and locked it.

The atmosphere inside the room was electric. Men stood there with water dripping off them from the pool. I had met them all before except one, but I recognised him immediately. He was a world-famous racing driver. The others were part of Peter's inner

99

circle, the men who were always around him. They had all transformed in seconds from laughing party-goers into a highly professional team.

All eyes were riveted on Peter. He spoke in his clipped commanding tone and, as always, he went straight to the point.

'The problem, Neil?'

'It's an A2 situation in R7.' Neil spoke to us in an unemotional monotone. 'We need information, and quickly.' He turned to Peter. 'Sunray will be calling you, sir, in about thirty minutes.'

I was not yet au fait with all the Department's codes, though I could guess what an A2 situation was. It must be top priority, I thought. Anyway, the atmosphere in the room and the expression on Peter's face told me so.

My brain seized on a random selection of possibilities. What was happening in the world at the moment, I asked myself? Was it another Russian sputnik overflying America on a spying mission? Or perhaps the reverse – another American U2 spy flight shot down in embarrassing circumstances that would inevitably be followed by another Gary Powers trade-off?

Was it another round of the Arab/Israeli war? Were the Chinese threatening to enter the Vietnam War? Perhaps another Communist coup in the Middle East or Africa? Or was there yet more trouble with Cuba? Could it be another nuclear confrontation with the Russians?

Alternatively, it could be something nearer home. Was it the Baader-Meinhof Gang at work in Germany once again? Or more trouble in Berlin, another Checkpoint Charlie situation? Maybe another Iron Curtain country was rebelling. Or had the world's number one terrorist, Carlos the Jackal, struck again?

Surely it wasn't another Communist mole in the

official Intelligence Services – the discovery of a 'fourth' man after the others? Or was it now the Americans' turn to discover one at the top of the CIA?

This flurry of possibilities passed through my mind in seconds. I looked up and saw that the team had broken into separate working units, with everyone busy. The room was buzzing with activity, and Neil was obviously the co-ordinator.

I looked across at Peter, who was standing back so that he could see and hear everything. Then he gave a curt nod to the racing driver, and the man walked over to a bookcase. He quickly scanned a section of it before taking out a large book. Then, reaching into the space left by the book, he pressed a button and the two central parts of the bookcase slid aside to reveal a large room. There, two operators wearing headphones were sitting in front of what looked like a huge radio set.

Within seconds, the room was transformed into a control centre.

Peter had told me there was a radio section in the safe house that operated twenty-four hours a day. So this was where Ian Fleming had hijacked some of his ideas!

The sound of the airwaves emanated from the radio as the operators tuned the controls, seeking the right frequencies and the best reception. To me it sounded like the noise a whale or porpoise might make – a kind of undulating wailing.

Up to this point I had stayed in the background. But now Peter's eyes swept the room before fastening onto me. He seemed to be thinking for a minute, then he said, 'Helen. Man the green phone on the desk over there. You are talking to London. Acknowledge the information, collate the data as it comes in and give me an overview when I signal you.'

'Yes, sir.'

I felt a frisson of terror. I'd never done anything like this before. Who was at the other end? What information were they going to feed in? Would I remember it accurately? I knew that people's lives and more could be dependent on my getting it right.

Then I realised: Peter trusted me to handle this. That gave me the confidence I needed.

I walked over to the phone and sat down on a chair. All my senses were alert as I waited for it to ring. Five minutes later it did. When I picked it up, I heard a bland, monotonous male voice at the other end. He gave me his identification and I responded with mine, which seemed to satisfy him.

'Mister Monotone' fed me non-stop information for the next thirty or forty seconds, occasionally going into code: 'SX is now at GH'. I was amazed at how much he managed to cram into so short a time. He signed off by saying 'I'll update again in seven minutes.'

'Acknowledged,' I said.

I had managed it!

I mentally filed all the information in preparation for the next calls. There were two more, both from Mister Monotone. The data was sufficient to tell me what was being done to meet the perceived threat and how the threat itself was unfolding.

Neil called for silence. Peter said, 'We have eight minutes before Sunray calls. Each section brief me on progress. Helen, you will go last.'

I felt nervous again. Would I get it right when it was my turn? How long would I have? I could have taken up the full eight minutes with my own data alone. I quickly tried to sort out the priorities. Thank goodness he hadn't asked me to go first!

In fact, when it came to my turn Neil helped me. 'You have one minute, Helen.'

I had been listening very closely to the others, which had made me sift through and re-group my information so that I only gave the relevant parts. I was surprised to find that it was easier that I had expected.

I had just finished when one of the operators on the radio called out: 'It's Sunray for you, sir, coming up by alternative means. Three minutes.'

Peter walked over to the phone. Everyone went very quiet. The phone shrilled, piercing the silence. It sounded harsh and demanding. Peter picked it up on the second ring.

'Yes, Mr President.'

I noted that he went into formal 'on parade' mode, a change from his usual informal relationship with such people. I watched his face as he listened intently to what was being said. From his replies, I realised this was the President of the United States.

After some three or four minutes he concluded their conversation. 'Yes, Mr President. I'll connect with Stansfield. Goodbye.'

Stansfield? Who was Stansfield? I wondered.

Peter signalled me to go over to him. He pointed me to a door leading into a small anteroom that overlooked the swimming pool.

'I'll be with you in a second,' he said as he walked over to Neil.

I sat down and looked out through the sun blinds at the party, which was now in full swing. The difference between the scenes on either side of the blinds was startling. Outside, I could see people who'd had too much to drink flirting with one another. Someone threw a girl into the swimming pool, fully-dressed, as people laughed. Inside, we were all in total control mode, geared perhaps towards the survival and protection of these very people. I realised that it was only because of our world inside that their world outside could exist so freely.

I didn't like what I saw on the other side of the blinds. This was part of the world Peter gave so much of himself for. Why did too much money and security seem to lead inevitably to boredom, dissolution and depravity? I thanked God for all the ordinary, decent people who often struggled to make ends meet and lived by solid, old-fashioned values.

I felt Peter's presence behind me and turned away from the window. He asked me some detailed questions about my phone calls and I told him everything I had heard in logical sequence. I had been anxious to get it right in my head as we were discouraged from writing anything down. If we did have to, it was always shredded before we left the room. There were to be no footprints in the sand and that rule was absolute. Peter knew that I assimilated information quickly and easily, and I now knew just how useful that was to the Department.

'What do your instincts tell you about the situation?' he asked me.

I was surprised, to say the least. He wanted an opinion from me!

'I think they're bluffing,' I said. 'They believe they have control and they're manipulating us. I think the Americans need to call their bluff – to face them down.'

Peter grew thoughtful. 'Hmm – yes, that was the President's view. I want one more piece of information, then we'll advise.'

'Is that what you're doing – advising the American President?'

'Yes, at the moment.' He smiled at me.

'I had no idea,' I said, 'how many air-bases the United States had over here. Listening to all this, I get the impression that we're barely more than an unsinkable aircraft carrier for the Americans, sitting off mainland Europe.'

'Yes, but it's necessary.'

'Why?'

'The possibility of the Russians over-running

Europe is very real. Unfortunately, we do not have the resources to protect ourselves.'

Just then a voice called across the room. 'The Admiralty, by alternative means, sir.'

The red phone rang and Peter picked it up. After exchanging courtesies he asked some questions. I didn't understand most of the conversation as it was coded.

'Thank you. Yes, that's all. Goodbye.'

The phone rang again almost immediately. Peter picked it up.

'Yes Mr President, my advice at the moment is ...'

The conversation between them seemed quite relaxed and it was obvious they knew each other well. Before Peter signed off I heard him say, 'Mr President, we'll remain on listening watch. I don't anticipate you and I will need to speak again until midnight our time. I will make sure the Prime Minister is informed when I return to London this evening.'

Goodness, I thought, this is high-powered stuff!

When Peter had replaced the receiver, he said, 'Okay everyone – stand down – thank you.' He walked over to the radio operators and gave them instructions before turning back to us. 'Come on, we must rejoin the party.'

We walked through a corridor and out onto the terrace. Again I saw just how expert Peter was at jumping from one role to another as he went straight into his playboy style, throwing himself into a chair alongside some giggling acquaintances who thought they were friends.

'Where have you two been?' one of them asked. 'We'd almost given you up for lost!' They giggled.

'Oh we were invited to a private viewing of a blue film. It got very boring and predictable towards the end.' Peter laughed. 'We both thought we'd prefer the company outside.' And he turned and signalled the waiter for drinks.

But I found it so difficult. I was standing there feeling lost when a lovely-looking girl sitting next to Peter looked up and addressed me.

'Does he belong to you,' she said, turning to grin at him, 'or can anyone try?'

I felt a stirring of irritation 'Oh, anyone can try,' I said casually and walked away. Imagine Peter belonging to anyone, I thought.

I went to the edge of the pool, threw off my towelling robe and dived in. I swam furiously. The physical exercise felt good and I must have swum five or six lengths. Then I jumped out at the far end, as far from the group as I could get. There, sitting on the grass, was the racing driver. He looked at me curiously.

'Well … hello.' He looked me up and down. 'How long have you been with Peter?'

I was wary. Although I'd only just met this man, I hadn't taken to him much. And questions now made me nervous.

'Nearly a year.'

'Good heavens! You've lasted a long time. What have you got that the others hadn't?'

Now I really didn't like him.

'I don't know – perhaps you should ask him.'

I turned and deliberately walked away. To my relief I saw Neil sitting on his own under the shade of a big tree. I liked Neil, and felt that in time we might even become friends. He was very close to Peter and I had empathy with him.

'Can I join you?' I asked.

He nodded with a smile; gratefully I sat down next to him. We didn't talk, each of us seeming to understand the other's need for silence. I felt sad, inadequate and very alone. At that moment I wanted to go home. I wanted to be with Peter, but not like this. I wanted to be alone with him, to talk to him, explain how I felt. I needed him to understand me as he had in Spain. I needed his help.

Looking across the pool at him, I saw that the girl who had spoken to me had obviously taken me at my word. She was standing, trying to pull Peter up from his chair and, laughing, he allowed her to. Putting her arms around his neck, she began flirting outrageously with him. She was exceptionally beautiful and I must have visibly flinched because Neil touched my arm.

'Don't worry – it means nothing.'

Just then I saw Peter push her long dark hair to one side and whisper something into her ear. She stepped back, stared at him open-mouthed, then flounced off. Peter laughed and sat down.

I sighed. Since I was getting chilly after my swim, I decided to go back into the house and change into my clothes. I managed to slip away without anyone noticing except Neil. They were all too busy having what they considered a good time.

After I had changed, I found myself inexorably drawn to the room where our meeting had taken place. Outside the door, I reached down and gently tried the handle, expecting it to be locked, but it opened under my touch. I went in very slowly, not knowing what to expect.

The room was empty, everything looked quite normal. There were no telephones and the bookcase was back in place. I walked over to it and listened for any sound behind: nothing.

It was as if the meeting had never happened. Then I saw three damp patches on the pale blue carpet and they were somehow reassuring. I sat down in a very large leather chair. It felt safe around me and I began to think about things.

My new life was, I decided, like being on a rollercoaster and I was really struggling with the highs and lows, the twists and turns. There was no safety bar and I was constantly at risk of being thrown out. When we went operational, I zoomed up onto a high.

I had felt that today, especially as I had really been able to contribute for the first time. But when we went back outside, I plummeted. From something so important to something so pathetic.

Shortly I would go home to the children. That was a different sort of high and necessitated a sharp turn on my part. I realised how tired I was, how easy it would be to just give up. If only there was someone to talk to, but there was no-one. There could be no-one. Yes, I could talk to Jessie – but not about the real difficulties I was having. I don't think I have ever felt so alone as I did at that moment.

The door opened. It was Peter. I stood up, so pleased to see him.

'What are you doing?' He was cold. My heart sank.

'I just wanted to get away from that – from them.'

'Why?'

'I – it was too big a jump, so quickly. I couldn't cope.'

He stared at me coldly. 'You have to cope, Helen – get out there now. Do you understand?'

I nodded. He left the room without a backward glance and once again, as on the first night I met him, I thought I hated him.

You cold bastard, I thought. Yet I knew I would do exactly as he said.

I walked back out to the party. When he saw me he nodded curtly.

For the next two hours I mingled, laughed, giggled, but all the time I felt dead inside. I hated all of it and all of them, and at that moment, all of it included him.

Eventually the last person left and I threw myself exhausted into a chair. Peter came up to me. I looked up.

'Leave me alone,' I said. He raised an eyebrow. 'I hate them all and I hate you too.'

'No you don't,' he smiled sardonically.

'You arrogant, conceited, superior bastard!' I shouted.

He laughed. 'Helen, you are wonderful when you're angry.'

'You arrogant, conceited, superior bastard!' I yelled again, as if the repetition would make him believe it.

He laughed even harder. I wanted to hit him but I hadn't the energy. Suddenly I found myself trembling and, afraid I was going to cry, I got up quickly.

'I'm just going to get my things,' I said and walked quickly towards the house, his laughter still echoing.

I went upstairs and collected my things. Slowly I began to calm down. I realised I was overtired and stressed, and I didn't really want to leave like this. I was still crazy about him. Sitting down, I took some deep breaths and concentrated on regaining control as Peter had taught me. Gradually it came.

Once I was calm, I began to understand what he had done. It was the way he always taught me and it was very effective, helping me to gain confidence and learn by experience. He had told me I had to cope and then left me; it was up to me to do it myself.

I was learning to know and control myself.

When I was ready I went back downstairs to where he was still sitting. He looked up and smiled questioningly.

'I just want to apologise,' I said quietly.

'What for? It's not appropriate. You haven't done anything wrong.'

'But I couldn't cope. Then I was so rude to you.'

'No, Helen, that is not so. You told me you couldn't cope, but then you did.' He looked at me gently. 'What you said to me is probably true. I think I am an arrogant, conceited bastard – even a superior one.' He smiled. 'Do you know just how beautiful and fearless you are when you are angry?'

Now I smiled, a trifle embarrassed. 'No.'

A look I recognised crossed his face; a look that told me that he wanted me.

'Come back with me tonight and stay a couple of days.'

Oh no! I thought. My mind flitted across all the reasons I couldn't go, but only one really mattered and that was the one I didn't want him to know about. I prevaricated.

'I'm afraid I can't. I have to take Jessie to Chester tomorrow.'

He stared at me intently. The seconds ticked by. I couldn't meet his eyes so I looked down.

'Come here.' His voice was quiet. I walked across to him, too tired to think of what to do. He took my chin in his hand and lifted my face gently until I was forced to look at him.

'Lying to me would be extremely dangerous.'

'I *have* promised to take Jessie to Chester tomorrow,' I insisted.

He stared at me again but then turned abruptly. 'I'll get them to bring your car round.' And he walked into the house.

I sighed with relief. Yes, I had promised to take Jessie to Chester, but I had also promised to take the children there, to the zoo. It wasn't a lie, more an evasion of the whole truth. The problem now was, would Peter leave it or would he dig further?

I knew I could never lie to him directly, but I was desperate not to be put in a position where he knew I was choosing between my love for him and my love for my children. I just denied that it could happen – by never allowing the problem to surface. I always made sure in advance that I knew what he expected of me: when he wanted to see me, for how long. This was the first time he had spontaneously changed our plans.

I knew why and I was flattered. I wanted to go with him very much, but my maternal instincts were stronger. The children needed consistency in their lives, they had to be sure that when I made a promise to them I would keep it. I knew I was their anchor, but what I didn't know at the time was that they were also mine.

Why didn't I just tell Peter the truth? It was complicated. I wasn't sure he would understand. I thought he would feel he was competing with my children. They came first and I wasn't at all sure he would accept that. I wasn't prepared to even consider the possibility of him finding out, so I risked being economical with the truth although I knew it was dangerous.

I tried to convince myself that he had believed me. How foolish I was! Peter knew the real reason I refused to go home with him, he just decided not to confront me at that time.

Just then my car appeared from around the corner, with Peter at the wheel.

'Come on, you're very tired,' he called. 'I shall drive you home.'

'But you have to be back in London this evening before midnight to make sure the Prime Minister is briefed. I'm holding you up.'

'There's no problem, Helen. I have my helicopter waiting to take me when I'm ready.'

So I jumped in and we left.

How organised this man's life was, I thought. How many people in positions of great power depended on him. How resolute and reliable he was. When it mattered, sleep was of no importance. A midnight briefing was no problem, neither was any other hour, or food or drink, or any other need or comfort. Everything was sacrificed in the service of his country.

On the way home I couldn't resist asking him,

'What did you say to that girl – the one who pulled you off the chair?'

'I told her to fuck off,' he said quite seriously.

I was shocked. Peter very rarely swore. He thought it disempowered people, and he loved the English language so much, he considered it lazy not to use it properly. He had never sworn at me.

'Why – what had she done?'

'She was playing games with me. I don't play games, Helen.'

No he didn't, that was for sure!

When I arrived home the children were in bed but still awake. Calling out to Jessie, 'Hello, I'm back. I'll just kiss the children good night', I ran up the stairs. They were not even sleepy, both squeaking with joy and excitement at the prospect of going to the zoo.

'Can Auntie Jessie come too?' they exclaimed.

'Of course she can, darlings. It's all arranged. Now good night, sleep tight.' I tucked them in and gave them both a big hug. Blowing them a last kiss at the door, I went downstairs.

Jessie was in the kitchen. 'You look tired,' she said. 'I'll put the kettle on. The children have been so good. We went for a walk in the forest.'

'Oh, thanks, Jessie. They love you so much, you know. You are coming to the zoo with us tomorrow, aren't you?'

'I wouldn't miss it for the world. Now, tell me, did you have a nice day?'

'Yes,' I said hesitantly.

'You don't sound so sure.'

I couldn't tell her everything, but I told her about the mood of the party and my distaste for some of the people there.

'I just wanted to be alone with Peter,' I added

wistfully. 'He asked me to go back to London with him tonight but I refused.'

'Darling, why didn't you go?'

'I'd promised to take the children to the zoo.'

'Goodness, what did he say? Did he mind?'

'I didn't tell him it was the children. I told him I had to take you to Chester.'

Jessie looked puzzled. 'Why didn't you tell him the truth? It was perfectly understandable.'

'I don't want him to even think about the children.'

'Why not? Why don't you bring him here to meet them?'

'No!' I realised I sounded horrified, and tried to lighten my tone. 'I just don't want him to get involved with them. He's totally dedicated to what he does, and he wouldn't have any time for them.'

Jessie stayed silent as I continued. 'The problem is, I don't think he believed me and I think he did mind. Oh, gosh, Jessie I hope he doesn't ask me about it again.'

'Well, it's a good thing I'm coming to the zoo with you,' she said and laughed. 'We must make sure we have a really good day. Let's take the little ones out for lunch as well.'

'I've an even better idea,' I said, catching her mood. 'I'll make one of my special "mummy picnics", and then they can run around freely in the gardens.'

Jessie nodded with approval. Then: 'Darling,' she paused thoughtfully, 'I don't think he believed you either but for some reason he chose not to take it any further – not for the time being anyway. I suspect he will one day so you should be prepared. Now, I must go. Don't run me home, I'll enjoy the walk. I'll see you tomorrow.'

After Jessie left I sat for a while pondering over what she had said. A warning bell rang in my head but, foolishly, I chose to ignore it.

## Chapter 12
## Headlines

Peter was not tolerant of mistakes. If you committed a stupid error, retribution was almost as swift and merciless as if you had done a deliberate wrong, and because of our closeness he was even harder on me. He was not interested in excuses; in his eyes there were no excuses. If you made a mistake, especially a serious one, you paid the price.

One day I made a mistake that was both stupid and serious.

I had gone for a country walk with the children and on returning to the car we saw a young man leaning against the door. He could not have been more than eighteen or nineteen, but he looked in a bad way. His hair was matted, he was very dirty and he had the red-raw eyes and pallor of someone who has not slept in days.

As he approached us, my first feeling was fear; was the man about to attack my children and me? But he could hardly stand and, as he began to speak in halting English, I realised he needed help.

And here, once again, the dichotomy of my life was thrown into relief.

For me, there was no alternative but to offer the man some kind of assistance. He was almost collapsing with fatigue and, no doubt, hunger, and I could not leave him there. If I had any reservations, my children's concerned faces soon squashed them. I had always tried to teach them to care for others, and this, of all situations, demanded compassion.

However, I was also involved in another world that could not afford to feel compassion. It would have been easier simply not to think about it too much, but I always did.

What I didn't think about was who this man might be.

As it turned out, he did need help, but in more ways than I realised: he was an illegal immigrant, newly arrived in England from Rumania.

Of course, initially I was blissfully unaware of his status and I took him home, fed him and made sure he saw a doctor. Fortunately, he did not stay long in my house, so my part in his story was over the minute he waved goodbye to the children and me – or so I thought.

Unfortunately, some members of the national Press were in the area at the time, having lunch in a nearby pub. The story they were working on was a long time developing and they were bored. The news of the immigrant – and my involvement – quickly circulated and two of the journalists decided to investigate. After a few enquires, they turned up at my door.

When they rang the bell and asked about the man, my first reaction was panic. Failure to hand over an illegal immigrant to the authorities was a serious offence; although I had genuinely not known, was I going to be in trouble?

I needn't have worried on that score. No, I wasn't in trouble, they said, but this was news and my family's unwitting part in it was an interesting angle. And, one of the reporters added, I was a photogenic subject, which always increased a story's interest-value. Would I mind having a chat, doing an interview? And when they asked if they could come back later to take some photographs of us all, when my daughter would be home from school, I readily agreed.

I should have known better.

Peter had warned us all about the dangers of any publicity, especially photographs which revealed our real names and identities. But for some reason this never entered my head, probably because I'd had little to do with journalists before and didn't recognise the dangers. Also, I must admit I was flattered and succumbed to the sweet taste of recognition.

I was about to break a cardinal rule: letting my personal needs take precedence over the Department.

It was a fine evening and by five o'clock the front lawn was crowded with cameras, equipment and journalists. The children thoroughly enjoyed all the attention and, if I'm honest, so did I. The photographers all promised to send me copies of their photographs and eventually everyone left.

The next day all the top papers carried the story, most of them with pictures. I received surprised phone calls from friends and relatives, and even a friend in Paris picked up a British newspaper and saw a picture of me staring out at her from page one.

It still hadn't occurred to me that I might have done something wrong and when the phone rang the next morning I picked it up, full of the joys of spring.

'This is Neil, Helen. Peter wants to see you immediately.'

The tone of his voice alerted me that all was not well.

'Is there something wrong?' I asked.

'I think you'd better just get here as quickly as possible. I can't say any more.'

I knew I'd get nothing else out of him, so I asked where I was to go. Neil told me Peter would be waiting at one of the 'safe' houses he used in the area, where I had been many times before. It would take me about twenty minutes to get there, so I left as quickly as possible.

I jumped into the car and as I drove I began to

think. What had I done wrong? I had no inkling of how serious the situation was.

I thought about the immigrant – but no, it couldn't be that. It never entered my head to worry about the publicity, the photographs and the revelation of my true identity, there, in every national newspaper, for everyone to see.

On arriving at the house I experienced for the very first time what it was like to be in serious trouble with 'the Boss'. Instead of going straight into him as usual, I was told to wait in the drawing room, opposite the study he always used.

The longer I sat there, the more nervous I became. I didn't need to ask whether I was 'on' or 'off' parade.

Neil came in. 'Will you go through to the study now.'

I walked to the door and knocked three times.

'Come in.'

I entered the room. Peter was sitting at a desk overlooking the driveway, reading some papers.

'Good morning, sir.'

I knew he was angry immediately. Just the way he lit his cigarette told me that.

He looked up but said nothing, barely acknowledging my presence. His face was mask-like but his eyes blazed with fury. I had never seen him so angry.

He looked back down at his desk and continued to read. Then, on the other side of the room, I spotted a table on which were spread out the previous day's newspapers, all turned to the pages featuring the articles and photographs of me and the children.

My heart began to sink as it slowly dawned on me just how serious my mistake had been. Then the penny dropped. How could I have been so stupid?

I stood waiting and after what seemed an age, Peter got up and came round from behind the desk. He sat back against the front of it, his hands gripping the edge on either side of him.

'What the hell did you think you were doing?' His voice was icy cold but with a fury that I felt was only barely contained.

'I'm sorry,' I whispered.

'Pardon?' he almost spat at me.

'I'm sorry.'

His response was like a slap across the face. It left me speechless and numb.

'How dare you apologise!'

And then he launched into what I can only describe as a verbal lashing, so painful it felt like being cut with a knife. It came at me from all angles and was far worse than any physical beating. He left no part of me unscathed, cutting through me with the precision of a surgeon who knew exactly how to peel back the emotions until they were raw, and then pierce the most vulnerable parts.

He left me shaking with shock and fear. Finally, he spoke.

'Well, say something.'

I couldn't. I was frozen and completely dumbstruck. Anyway, there was nothing to say. He didn't want an apology – it was not enough and I couldn't think of anything that would be.

But after a while, from somewhere, some hesitant words began to come.

'I realise, sir, that an apology is not good enough. I don't know what else to say. I have no excuse to give you.'

'You're damned right you have no excuse. You pandered to your own ego and put it before the Department. Tell me – how did you think I was going to react to this?'

I couldn't look at him, I felt so ashamed. 'I didn't think, sir.'

I heard him cross the room.

'Look at me, Helen.' I looked up. 'At this moment I could surely kill you.'

I said nothing, but images of the man in the cell at Strangeways flashed through my mind. I could see him again and smell his fear. But this time it was me in the cell and I knew from experience that the man in front of me now was capable of carrying out his threat.

Time stopped. Like an animal transfixed by a car's headlights, I could do nothing but wait, paralysed by fear.

Peter came up very close to me and took my chin in his left hand. He lifted my face until I was forced to look into his eyes.

'Why don't you cry, Helen?'

I said nothing.

'Answer me – why don't you cry?' His hand gripped my chin harder.

'It wouldn't help,' I gasped.

'Suppose I want you to?'

He reached round behind me and with his other hand pushed my arm up my back into an armlock.

'I can't. Do whatever you have to, but I can't cry.'

As these words spilled out, it was brought home to me again that I was inexorably linked to this man in some primeval way. I couldn't explain it but it had been so since that night in Marbella. If he was going to kill me now, I would let him. I would not beg or plead and I would not cry.

Paradoxically, it was my willingness to let him kill me that probably saved my life.

I stood there waiting.

Slowly, with my one arm locked behind my back and his other hand under my chin, he pushed me back against the wall.

I said nothing. I waited. More images flashed by.

When he pushed my arm further up my back, the pain was intense.

'Cry, damn you, cry!'

I knew instinctively not to, and if I had I'm certain it would have been lethal. Peter would have instantly lost any remaining respect he had for me and disposing of me would have been much easier. I recalled the contempt on his face when the man in the cell had started whimpering; it had only made him more implacable, more deadly.

Without warning he released me, turned away and walked back to his desk.

'Get out and wait in the next room.'

He moved as if to sit at the desk, but I didn't move. He looked surprised.

'You heard me, Helen. Go and wait next door.'

It was as if I had been taken over by someone else and I heard my voice say quite clearly, 'No, sir, I won't cry and I won't wait in the next room.'

Another part of me decided that I had gone quite, quite mad but the part that was now in charge was very definite.

I saw a look of curiosity pass across his eyes but his voice was angry. 'Why not?'

I didn't know why not, and at this point I decided I was completely insane.

'I think you know what you want to do, sir. Why don't you do it?'

'That is incredibly presumptuous. How dare you tell me what I want to do!'

I said nothing.

'But you're right, Helen – I know exactly what I want to do and I intend to do it.'

He walked over to the door and locked it.

He turned and sat again on the front of his desk. There was a deathly silence. I could hear a clock ticking somewhere. It seemed to get louder and louder in my head. I tried to work out why I was being so dangerously foolhardy. Why had I disobeyed him? I knew better than that. I was obviously in the clutches of some part of me that was incapable of accepting the inevitable.

Well, it was too late now.

What did I expect him to do about someone who had the audacity not only to disobey him, but to answer back and even tell him what to do?

I looked up at him, and couldn't believe what I saw.

He was grinning and, at the look of astonishment on my face, he burst out laughing.

'You stupid girl. You stupid, brave, silly girl.'

I smiled, then I laughed. Before long we were both convulsed as the tension in the room evaporated and our taut emotions dissolved into mirth.

It was these extremes in Peter that made him so endlessly fascinating. I had first experienced such extremes in my own father, who could range from gentleness at one end of the emotional spectrum to ruthlessness at the other. As I adored my father, this had always attracted me – but in him, as in other men I have met, the extremes were balanced by all the emotions in between.

With Peter, there were no in-between emotions because his life had no middle ground. He was either loving and warm, or cold, clinical and ruthless. In all aspects of his life, he was either at one end of the scale or the other, which made him complex and potentially dangerous if one became emotionally involved with him. Combined with his attractiveness, it had left a lot of women before me hurt, even devastated.

But, because of my father, I loved and understood men of extremes. I wanted to understand Peter more and once I saw the lack of middle ground, it became easier. Coping with the massive emotional swings was difficult but thrilling. It made me love him more.

This intemperance had shocked a close mutual friend one night. The three of us were having drinks, and I had gone out of the room to make a phone call. Noticing our closeness, the friend had remarked to Peter quite innocently, 'You really care about Helen, don't you?'

Peter picked up his wine glass and hurled it across the room. It hit the far wall where it smashed into smithereens, leaving a dark ugly stain on the wallpaper.

'I can't afford to care about anyone,' he snarled. 'Good night!'

Then he picked up his coat, walked purposely out of the room and out of the house.

When I returned, our friend was visibly upset. It was so out of character for the Peter he knew to show strong emotions, and it had really shocked him. But after he had told me what had happened, I knew there was nothing I could say to explain. I just smiled sadly and helped him clear up the mess.

I left shortly after and followed Peter home, knowing that once again he was fighting his feelings for me. It had happened many times before when we were alone together but this was the first in front of someone else, and the violence of his action had frightened me.

I rang the doorbell and Paul let me in. 'The Boss doesn't want to be disturbed,' he told me, but did not stop me as I headed for the stairs.

My heart sank. This was not going to be easy. Slowly I climbed the stairs. The double doors to the drawing room were firmly closed. I knocked gently. There was no reply, so I went in. Peter was sitting in his normal place on the Chesterfield, staring into the fire. He didn't look up.

'If you don't want to get hurt, Helen, get out.'

I thought about that and decided to stay. For me, leaving was not an option. And, despite what he said, I suspected it would not go down well with him either. I felt I was being challenged.

I went back to my childhood – my father coming back from work after a bad day, my mother telling me to leave him alone, but I wouldn't.

Now, with Peter, I did exactly what I had done with my father all those years ago. I walked slowly across the room and sat down quietly on the floor at his feet with my back resting on the arm of the Chesterfield. I was close enough to touch him but I was careful not to. I said nothing.

Looking at the carriage clock on the mantelpiece, I noted it was nearly midnight. When I looked again, twenty minutes had passed. When I had first sat down, he had tensed and I thought he was going to move but he didn't. Gradually, even though I couldn't see him, I felt him relax.

Then, just like my father, his hand came down, first on my shoulder and then he stroked my cheek. I continued to sit quietly at his feet. I knew I could sit there in silence as long as was necessary. After all, I had done it many times as a child. I used to call it 'communing with my father'. Now I was communing with Peter.

Then he spoke. 'Helen, if you choose to stay in my life, ultimately you will be hurt.'

His tone was non-threatening, the words came across as a simple statement of fact. I turned to look up at him.

'I know,' I said as gently as I could, and rested my hand on his knee. 'But I'm not going anywhere unless you make me. Whatever happens, happens.'

He sighed and smiled at me.

That night was the first time I saw that I could help him. Love was an emotion he had no idea how to handle, and I learned later that he had never experienced it as a child, whereas I had. I knew that he could teach me many things, but perhaps I could teach him that it was safe to love. I might get hurt along the way, but it would be worth it.

That night my love for him matured.

I never courted publicity again and even now I am wary of the Press. They have an important job to do and on the whole they do it well, with sympathy and good taste. Occasionally their methods are distasteful but in my case, what happened was entirely my own fault.

I am against a privacy bill or any law that would restrict the freedom of the Press. Any such law or bill would mainly protect the wrong people – those in positions of power and privilege, those in public office. These are the very people who, because of their position, must be accountable for their behaviour and standards.

Luckily there were no repercussions for the Department, or me, as a result of this incident. But I still have some wonderful photographs of us all which, true to their word, the newspapers sent me.

Enough said.

## Chapter 13
## The Department

Up to this time, I had not really been aware of exactly how the Department worked. Peter had instigated a superb system, and now he decided it was time for me to understand a little more. He sat me down one day and began to explain.

'When, as a young man, I established the Department, I recruited other wealthy and influential men into it. They lead their own lives but they also help the Department. Their contributions are very different. These people usually come from the aristocracy or middle classes: landowners, businessmen, politicians, professional men – in short, men with power and ability. All of them do what they do out of the same motivation – a profound love for their country.'

The men Peter gathered around him within his 'inner circle' were all patriots. Considering their already successful lives, there was no other reason for them to become involved. They offered the Department their services and resources – resources such as helicopters, ships, aircraft, advance communications, as well residences for use as safe houses and so on.

This inner circle consisted of only a few people but they were all above average in intelligence, in fact often brilliant, which they had already proved in their own fields. Peter chose the people he approached very carefully, and they were always thoroughly investigated before being recruited.

'Another group within this inner circle,' Peter said,

'are my own personal staff. Ostensibly, they are employed as my chauffeur, butler, valet and so on, but they are actually my ADCs, always available, day and night, totally committed to me personally. These were the men you saw with me in Spain.'

Ah, I thought. I had described them then as his entourage, the moths round the flame of a wealthy playboy. These men were all younger than Peter, and skilled at appearing to be shallow hangers-on, just living off him. In time I got to know some of them well. Paul and Neil, in particular, accepted me quite quickly and I ultimately counted them as my friends.

I soon realised that they were special and devoted their lives, in equal measure, to Peter and Great Britain.

So this was the inner circle – thirty or forty people who knew what Peter really did. In that elite group, of which I became a member, only I knew his real identity.

The actual executive consisted of seven or eight people taken from one or other of the two groups, depending on requirements. But the final decisions were ultimately made by Peter.

He explained, 'I am the only direct contact with the heads of the official Intelligence Services and the heads of the Armed Forces, the Police and the Civil Service. I have direct access to the most powerful and influential people in the world – presidents, prime ministers and heads of state.'

He paused. I knew all this already, as I had seen him pick up the phone and speak to these luminaries as equals, often just informing them of what he intended to do, more out of courtesy than 'need-to-know'. There was never a hint of sycophancy in his voice, and I don't think it ever occurred to him that some of them might have thought themselves his superior. He just didn't think that way: he expected mutual respect and co-operation and he got it.

Seeing and hearing this did wonders for my own

self-confidence and when I met people in elevated positions, I behaved in the same way, thrilled when it inspired the same result.

Peter continued: 'In the next circle around this inner core are the "connectors". These men are briefed by one of the inner circle and never meet me. They don't know me, they probably don't even know I exist. In fact, they rarely know one another. If they do meet it is a one-off. Their only contact is one of the inner circle, and it would always be the same one.

'This is the first of the absolute cut-offs. However, at this level they do know that they are part of a special section of the Intelligence Services.'

Peter told me that the connectors rarely did the actual operations. That job went out to the next circle – the operators. These were the thousands of men and women, most of them with ordinary jobs and lives, who were prepared and willing to help, as and when required. The operators were briefed by one of the connectors. Each had his or her area of operations and only knew their connector as a name. They were aware that they were helping the Intelligence Services, but they knew nothing about the Department.

'This is why the Press, on occasion, quote MI5 or MI6 legitimately denying involvement with something or someone. It will be something or someone they do not wish to know about or to associate themselves with, and it is right that this is so.'

Then Peter grew philosophical. How could a democratic nation, he asked me, defend itself against evil, when evil has such different rules? How did one fight anything so repugnant?

'How *do* you?' I asked.

He frowned. 'Let's look at this hypothetically. In those circumstances, one might have to throw away the rule book, but that would never absolve one from being accountable for one's actions. One would have to be able to justify each deed, not only to oneself but to the British people.

'In World War Two, for example, "Bomber" Harris could justify the destruction of the Ruhr armaments industry because that was the means by which the Germans were keeping the war going. But he could not justify the destruction of Dresden just before the end of the war. His motive there was pure vengeance. He was supping with the devil. With this action he tainted himself and the British people, and neither they nor history will ever forgive him.'

He gave me a meaningful look. 'If one found that one had to sup with the Devil, better to do it with a long spoon. In supping with the Devil, one must never be tainted by him. Integrity is sacrosanct.'

So, if one had to breach the rules, Peter seemed to be saying, one had to be sure of one's motive. That applied to anyone who was involved in intelligence work.

'So how would one sup with the Devil without becoming tainted by him?' I asked innocently. He raised one eyebrow – a warning signal not to ask any more questions.

So I tried to work it out for myself. I wondered if there was another 'outside' circle that could be used if the rules had to be broken. Sadly, there are men and women everywhere who will do anything for the right price. Their only motive is hard cash, and they are drawn by adverts or word of mouth, promising payment for certain services rendered. They are often ex-criminals, con-men, mercenaries, ex-military personnel, or anyone else looking for a quick buck. They usually have no idea who they are doing the 'job' for, and they are expendable.

I suspect that, when necessary, intelligence services all over the world use such people. And, despite our higher motives, I suspect we used them too.

As I came to understand the way the Department worked, I began to question where the man in the Strangeways cell fitted in. I doubted he had been an operator, as there seemed to be too many cut-offs. Operators only ever met one 'connector', and he was just a name to them. Even when the connectors said they worked for MI5 or MI6, this was almost always greeted with amused disbelief, and anyway, it was deniable. Obviously it was possible an operator could bungle an operation, although some of them were only used for information-gathering.

The man in the cell could have been one of the few superb, experienced operators who did the most demanding work, but even then, he would have had little opportunity for betrayal, for he would not have known *who* to betray.

So I decided he was most probably a connector. That would definitely have been more serious, as he would have had access to at least one person within Peter's inner team, someone invaluable to the Department and possibly in the public eye. He would then have had the opportunity to sabotage an entire operational mission.

Yes, I reasoned, he was either a top operator or a connector who double-crossed the Department, which would also explain why Peter had dealt with him personally. Peter's loyalty to his inner circle was absolute – and so was his fury if one of them was betrayed.

I decided to ask Peter. After all, we had a contract. He would either tell me the truth or decline to answer.

He declined to answer, except to say quietly, 'It's better for you, Helen, if you never know.'

I was not surprised. I had noticed how Peter was very protective of his people. Time and again he would carry the burden of a decision or a piece of knowledge, not sharing the pain or responsibility with anyone.

I knew how much it took out of him because now he allowed me to stay overnight and sometimes he would be off guard. Then I would see him exhausted, unable to sleep because of anxiety over an operation. I would see him trying to reconcile himself to some decision that had already been taken, or which was irreconcilable. Sometimes he reached a limit of human endurance beyond my comprehension.

This was the agony of a man whose value system was tested to breaking point. He would smoke incessantly and prowl around the house, unable to settle to anything. He wouldn't eat but would constantly sip at a drink. I longed to be able to help him but felt the frustration of knowing there was nothing I could do.

He explained to me that he needed that tension, needed to be on edge. If I had tried to relax him I could have blunted the razor-sharp thinking and lightning reactions that were essential to his work.

So I helped him by just being there and accepting his state of mind. I was complimented and flattered that now he never asked me to leave. I knew that he valued my presence and my silence.

At such times I guarded him jealously and his closest circle learned to trust me and even Paul and Neil, when I asked them to, would follow my instructions. Our roles would then reverse and Peter would allow me to be in control. He would talk to me about how he felt and that was when I came closest to this man, and when I realised the sacrifices he had made: never to be able to love or care for a woman, or allow a woman to love him; never to marry, have children, nurture them and watch them grow; in short, never to live in the real world.

I would gently massage his shoulders and eventually he would sleep. I would sit close to him as he drifted off, watching the hard tension lines disappear from his face. It would smooth and relax and I would feel an overwhelming love for him. Sometimes I would then slip into the bed beside him, cuddle up and fall asleep myself. At others I would sit in the chair and watch him until he awoke. When he saw me his face would crease into a smile and I could be sure the worst was over.

On a couple of occasions I suggested that perhaps he could share his burden with one or two of the others, but his answer was always the same. 'No – it has to stay with me. No one else must carry it.'

Except for Neil and maybe Paul, I don't think the others around him had any idea of what he went through. On one occasion he had to make a horrendous choice which involved a child. He agonised for hours, knowing he had a deadline for the decision. When that time arrived, he told the two people involved to go ahead.

'What about the child, sir?'

'The child is of no consequence,' he replied coldly.

I saw the look pass between the two as Peter left the room.

'Christ!' said one, 'that man has a stone where his heart should be. I know it's the right decision but ...' And he shook his head.

They looked across at me.

'How wrong you are,' I said, but I could say no more.

Peter was the epicentre of all the circles. Everyone and everything else radiated out from him, orbited around him, and it was his energy that fuelled us all.

If ever this country had a modern unsung hero, then this was he. Here was a man who had sacrificed all personal needs, and who never needed, sought or received credit for anything he did. That would go to the official Intelligence Services, and if any did come his way he would bat it back. After all, the Department didn't exist, so it certainly couldn't get recognition.

Peter saw ego as a weakness that could quickly and easily be exploited by others – an Achilles heel that could put everything at risk. Most if not all of us have a craving to satisfy our egos. Peter's strength lay in recognising the dangers and denying his ego, and this was paramount to his success as a leader, and for the Department.

It was enough for him that he did it.

But for me it wasn't. During one of my vigils, when I sat watching this man and the price he was paying for our freedom, I vowed that one day this country and the whole world would know about him. But I also vowed that I would never damage or put at risk the work he did.

It is only now, when sufficient time has passed since the existence of the Department, that I feel able to tell his story.

Peter had immense power and powerful friends. He needed that power. Our country, Great Britain, was being suffocated by more and more bureaucracy. We were determined to play cricket – after all, we were the modern parents of democracy – but others were not. They played by their own rules, they had no integrity. Peter understood that you can't play cricket when your opponents are playing street games.

There is a stereotype of a Head of Intelligence; and a man courting dubious publicity, throwing himself into the limelight of London society, mixing with the over-wealthy and often decadent types that frequented places like the Clermont Club is its very antithesis.

But that is exactly what Peter did. He didn't mind that his public image was quite frankly that of a *roué* who ponced about London, being seen at all the gambling and nightclubs with a succession of female social butterflies; or at all the annual social events like Ascot, Henley and the Derby with the flavour of the month on his arm. People fawned over him, and it reminded me of a decadent French court.

If I wanted to be with him at these times, I had to immerse myself in this milieu as well, which meant working out my own act. The only way I found I could do it was by pretending to be a naive and rather empty-headed 'Daddy's girl'. I learned to giggle and be coy, to feign ignorance or an inability to understand things, to appear amused by everything and everyone. I pretended not to notice the occasional patronising looks or behind-the-hand comments. I learned to hide the signs that might indicate inner strength or a will of my own. It was enough in these circles that I was glamorous, and I flaunted that to the full.

Eventually it became as easy as putting on my make-up, but there was a price to pay. For me that price was always the same – the feeling of isolation and, at worst, depression

Peter was unaffected by these people and situations. He had no need to be liked, never courted approval, and he was indifferent to people's opinions of him.

Reality for me was very different. I hated it all, and was always torn between wanting to be with Peter and detesting being with people I despised, acting out a part that offended me.

At one party Peter and I went to together, I nearly gave myself away. The man who had been seated next to me at dinner was the very worst example of the kind of person we mixed with. He behaved in a louche manner from the moment we sat down, and before long I felt his hand go up my skirt to rest on my upper thigh.

The first time he did it I remained in my role; I giggled and removed his hand, whispering, 'Now, now!' Of course it had no effect and his hand returned. What made it worse was that he totally ignored me and started a conversation with the man on my other side.

After removing his hand at least three more times, my real self could take no more. With my fork, I deftly stabbed the man's hand and he jumped, letting out a sort of squeal. There was a silence and everyone stared at us. Then, at Peter's warning glance, my false persona reappeared.

My reaction quickly put a stop to my table companion's behaviour but I could see he was baffled by it. However, he soon transferred his attentions to the girl on his other side, who seemed to thoroughly enjoy them.

Unbelievably, in the midst of all this shallow social whirl, Department business was sometimes transacted. Vital messages were sent, innuendos might have several levels of meaning, even glances could be covert signals.

We were not the only people in our circle who were not what we seemed. Some of the so-called shallow individuals were involved in the work of the Department and I learned that their contributions were priceless. The British have always been good at this kind of subterfuge, which was all part of the modus operandi of the Department. Even though I disliked it, I became a vital part of it. I could have done little else, standing as I did right next to the king.

Over the years, he began to draw me in. He sought my views and spent long hours questioning and examining them. At first I was tentative, but as he encouraged me I began to give more. Although I had initially worried about the diversity of my ideas, I soon realised Peter valued that. He used me to gain different perspectives on people and events and I stopped being afraid to suggest things in case they sounded stupid. They seldom did, and even if they had, he would take them anyway and weigh them up against his own ideas.

Peter was not a man who scoffed or put others down. He had no need to; he was the most naturally confident person I have ever met.

The night I broke his cover Peter had told me he needed and could use my talents in the Department. Now he was asking me to hone and apply them to the full, and I was responding with enthusiasm. I became more and more confident and with his open encouragement I would even interrupt him and throw in ideas of different ways we could do something. He would question me on the 'what' and 'why', and then we would discuss the 'how'.

The whole experience was energising and invigorating, and we often ended up sparking off each other like electrodes.

Now I felt I belonged to the Department. Now at last I felt I was one of them.

# Chapter 14
# Live With Me

I should not have been surprised at what happened next – after all, Jessie had indirectly warned me of it often enough.

'Helen, darling,' she would say in her gentle manner, 'relationships, once they've started, have a beginning, a middle and an end. Where is yours going with Peter?'

'I don't know,' I would say.

'You don't want to know, do you?' she replied.

Jessie would say no more, just smile kindly.

She must have brought up the subject at least half a dozen times over the years, but I chose not to think about it. Sometimes the question of where my relationship with Peter was heading would come into my head unbidden, but I dreaded trying to answer it, even though I knew I should.

Then the day arrived when I was forced to face it head on, with no preparation.

'Helen, I want you to come and live with me.'

I heard the words but somehow my brain didn't register them properly.

Early that morning I had caught the train to London, then jumped in a taxi at Euston and asked the cabbie to take me through Hyde Park. It was a typical spring day in England: the sun was shining and from the taxi I took in the beauty of the horse-chestnut trees with their pink blossom like ringlets on a beautiful girl. Riders were out exercising their horses, ducks flew off the Serpentine and Londoners were out in force enjoying the lovely weather. I felt as if I was dancing on air, happy to be alive. The daffodils in the park danced with me as they caught the breeze.

When I arrived at Peter's house I jumped out of the taxi, paid the driver and flew up the steps to the front door. I couldn't wait to see him, to be with him.

And now ... this.

His voice penetrated my thoughts. 'Well, what do you say?'

I looked up, startled. 'What do you mean?'

'I want you to come and live with me here in London.'

'But – I don't understand – I mean – how could I?'

'Quite simple, Helen. Just do it.'

I heard the cold edge in his voice. My brain was now racing, trying to sort out where I was with this, how I felt. After all, wasn't this what I had always wanted? So why was I hesitating?

My voice was speaking but I felt detached from it. I wanted to say 'No, don't say that' but it was out before I could stop it.

'What about the children?'

'What about them?'

'They couldn't live here.'

'Why not?'

His answers came at me fast, almost before my questions got out. I was even more confused.

'I don't know, I don't understand ...' My voice petered out.

He stared at me, his eyes narrowing. All the joy I had felt just a few minutes earlier now seemed like bubbles that burst as I tried to catch them. I wanted to leave the others safely suspended in the air, catching the light, but he wouldn't let me.

'What don't you understand, Helen?'

I shook my head. The bubbles burst around me. Why wouldn't he leave me alone?

'I don't know. What about the children? They couldn't live here,' I repeated miserably.

I looked about the beautiful, impeccably ordered room. It was so unsuitable for two young children. Everything, the whole situation was unsuitable.

'I would convert the top floor of the house and employ a full-time nanny. Of course, very shortly they will be going away to school. You wouldn't have to worry about them.'

I was stunned, shocked. As the final bubbles burst, reality loomed.

'So?' He walked up to me.

I turned away and went over to the window. The square below was bathed in that special green unique to spring – crisp, lush, with a sharp edge to it that mellows all through the summer into autumn softness. I wanted to go back into that spring sunlight, into my feelings of happiness before I had entered this room. I didn't want to have this conversation. I resented the disappearance of my beautiful bubbles.

'Please, Peter,' I appealed to him, 'please, I need time to think about this.'

'Why?' He was relentless.

'I need time. Please, just give me time.'

'OK.' His voice was like a pair of castanets, clicking out the words. 'OK. Take time. Go! Take time.'

He walked out of the room without even a backward glance and shut the door.

I picked up my jacket and small suitcase and went out of the house into the spring sunlight. I instinctively turned towards the centre of London and walked, realising that there were tears on my cheeks. But they were gentle and created no sense of hysteria, just an immense feeling of sadness.

I had always been aware of the danger to our relationship if I ever put Peter in a situation where his love for me came into conflict with his love for the

Department. I had been incredibly careful not to let such a situation arise. What I had not foreseen was the equal danger of him putting me in a situation where my love for him came into conflict with my love for my children. I had not prepared myself for that, had denied the possibility of it ever happening. After all, hadn't I made every effort to keep these two worlds separate?

Jessie had warned me that, one day, the issue of the children was one that Peter would make me confront. 'So you should be prepared,' she said. But I wasn't.

I walked slowly. Nobody paid me any attention and I took comfort in that. I could stay with my thoughts and feelings, allow myself to indulge them.

Little feet and little hands; calls in the night; tears that could easily be kissed away; feelings of love and tenderness that were so strong they were gut-churning. The smell, the feel, the touch of a child that was yours. The mind-blowing experience of motherhood. The knowledge that I had already left one man because he had hurt one of my children, and the absolute certainty that I would never let another man do the same – even if, especially if, that hurting took the form of denying their existence, seeing them as no more than some trivial nuisance that could be dealt with by 'Nanny' and boarding school.

Of course, I also knew one of my children was his child. If we moved in with Peter, he might start asking questions. There was a strong possibility that he would find out. Then what would happen? He might favour his son. Or he might reject him. They were both mine and I loved them equally. Because of security, they would have to be protected if we lived with Peter. They would be unable to grow up as normal children, and I could never risk that. They were the most precious things in my world.

My love for my children was an instinct that was primitive in its intensity. It transcended everything. Not even Peter could compete – no man could.

But my heart was breaking. I knew for sure how much it must have cost him to ask me to live with him. It was an open admission to the world of how much he cared. Basically it meant that love had won over his immense self-control and training; not the things he naturally guarded against – money, power, sex – but love, the one thing he believed he was impervious to.

The woman in me also knew that he would come to resent the victory of love. After all, he had always won battles before and over the months I had become resigned to him pushing me back and away from him when he sensed he was losing control.

Now, finally, love appeared to have won, but I was not so sure. This was the power of his love – versus the force of his will.

Every instinct in me told me it was incredibly dangerous. He had warned me that ultimately I would get hurt.

I walked. A police car passed, its siren blaring. A tramp lay sleeping on a bench in the sun. The daffodils continued their dance in the breeze, but I was no longer in tune with them.

I walked on until I found myself in Park Lane outside the massive new Hilton Hotel. Feeling tired, I went inside and took the lift up to the roof-top restaurant. It was very quiet and I ordered a pot of coffee. As I sat down, the decision I had made clicked and then locked firmly into place. I knew it was right and at least the certainty of that calmed me.

'Hello, Helen.'

I looked up. It was Neil. Of all the people in Peter's

inner circle, he was the one I was closest to. I was pleased to see him.

'Neil! Oh hello! What are you doing here?'

'Following you.' He smiled and sat down.

My heart leapt. 'Why are you following me?'

'Because that's what I'm assigned to do.' The tone was neutral but the eyes were kind.

'I don't understand.'

'Helen, I was there in Spain years ago, and you came under surveillance from that moment. I've been watching you ever since.'

'But – but, you're always with Peter.'

'Come, come! You know the system. I briefed the connector in your area, he then briefed operators as and when they were needed. Since then the Boss has always been, and still is, aware of your circumstances, and looking out for your safety and well-being.'

'Why?' I cried, more out of a need for reassurance than for actual information.

Neil paused, screwing his eyes up in reflection. I knew how loyal he was, first and foremost to Peter and then to the Department. I could see his mind working as he made a decision.

He began to talk. His voice was soft and gentle, so unlike Peter's. In the next hour Neil all but completed the jigsaw puzzle for me.

In the next hour Neil became my friend.

## Chapter 15
## Neil

'He loves you, Helen.'

'Does he?' My voice sounded petulant.

Neil's hand came across and covered mine. 'Listen,' he said firmly. He sat back and reflected for a moment, then he continued in a quiet, clear voice.

'I remember so well when we first saw you in Marbella. You were sitting on a bar stool, wearing a very short white dress, and your long bare legs were entwined around the stool. Peter was looking at you and he turned to me and said, "Hey, Neil – look at her!" It was man's talk and I knew him well enough by then to know exactly what he meant. I also knew that if he bothered to try for you he would probably succeed, and it would mean nothing to him. I was envious.

'I was in awe of the way he could attract women. He made it look so easy and I tried to copy him but his tactics were never so successful for me. Even though I employed exactly the same ones, he had something I didn't, a charismatic power. I would watch fascinated. I was even more fascinated when I realised it was all just a game. No woman ever got near him. He wined and dined them, charmed them, used them and then left – sometimes after one night, sometimes after a few weeks, but never more than a couple of months. However he was involved, he just extricated himself and left. I don't believe he wanted to hurt them. He just knew he couldn't get involved, and his control was absolute. He was an expert at saying no to himself ... until he met you.

'I knew very early on that you were going to be different. I knew in Marbella. Not the night we arrived. Then, you were just another beautiful girl he fancied. But the night you left, I knew you had really reached him in some way. I was both fascinated and worried. The Department could not afford this because Peter *was* the Department and it was essential that he was single-minded. A passing fancy was no problem but any real involvement with a woman was something else.

'We were expecting to stay for another week but on the day you left, he announced we were going back to London and told me to make arrangements. When we got back he briefed me to set up the normal procedures to watch someone. I was not surprised when that someone turned out to be you.

'Over the next twelve months I reported to him regularly on the constant flow of information I received. By the time he saw you again, Helen, he knew everything – *everything* – about you. That's how it has continued, and that's why I am here with you now.'

I looked at Neil, knowing every word he said was true. More pieces of the jigsaw slotted neatly into place and now a picture was beginning to emerge.

'He started seeing you again,' Neil continued. 'Over the next few weeks, in spite of what I had seen in Marbella, I believed – or maybe hoped – that he would finally tire of you as he had of the others. Most of them were a certain type, one that fitted his cover – young, beautiful social butterflies, girls who came up to London to do the season, to be seen. They flitted around the capital looking for excitement and, eventually, a wealthy husband. They clustered around Peter like moths round a flame and always got burnt. They were empty-headed and shallow, vain, spoilt and ambitious – I don't think they were too difficult for a

143

man with Peter's experience to resist. Of course he enjoyed bedding them, but that was all. I never saw one of them ever get close to him. He appeared completely impervious to love.

'The weeks passed into months and I became concerned. It wasn't personal, Helen. I liked you immensely. You were different from the rest, and in many ways, I could see how good you were for him. But I was concerned both for him and the Department because I couldn't see how it could ever work.

'I watched him fight his growing feelings for you, watched him hurt you and try to destroy what you had together. Sometimes I thought he had succeeded, but then your gentleness and understanding would captivate him all over again. I worried where it would all end.

'Then, as you know, it all came to a head the day he found out you knew who he was. I was at Heathrow that day, waiting to go with him to America. After waiting an hour I received a message to return to London immediately. When I arrived I walked straight into the middle of an unholy row. Sir Max, Sir John and Peter were really going at it. They had responded to my knock at the door, but then they ignored me.

'I could see you in the next room through the one-way mirror. You were sitting on a chair, looking pale and thoughtful. Obviously you couldn't hear the cacophony of noise in our room.

'The three of them were standing in the middle of the floor, shouting at each other. That in itself was highly unusual. I had never seen Peter so emotionally charged. It took me a few minutes to pick up what they were shouting about– it was you.

'When I realised what had happened, I was shocked. Sir Max and Sir John were adamant: you had broken Peter's cover and had to be eliminated. It was as simple as that. But Peter was fighting for your life and he was putting everything on the line.

'The force of his feelings was plain to see, and I realised then, for the first time, that he was deeply in love with you, and also deeply committed to you. So did everyone else in that room, including Peter himself. He had, for the first time, come face to face with that fact. I think he was shocked at the realisation, shocked at what he heard himself saying.

'He was telling them where they could put the Department, and all sorts of other things as well. Behind the words I heard the message: "If you want to kill her, then you'll have to kill me too." The power of that kept coming through everything he said. I felt desperate and considered whether to intervene, but I thought better of it. What could I say? What could I do? So I decided to rely on the immense mutual respect and trust that I knew these three men had for each other. I decided to wait. I stood back and listened.

'Suddenly, there was a pause. It seemed like the longest pause in the world. I watched Peter take absolute control of himself. He walked over to the wall, stood facing it, then he raised his clenched fists against the wall. We all watched as gradually he opened his hands flat. He turned slowly and deliberately to face us. His features were a mask and then they softened. He began to talk in a clear quiet voice. As he talked, he metamorphosed in front of my eyes into someone I had never seen before.

'He talked about you: his belief in you, his wonder of you. He talked about your courage, your spirit, your intelligence. He talked about your integrity and your strength of character. And as he talked the tension in the room lessened.

'I was mesmerised, so were the others. The way he spoke of you was beautiful. The expressions he used, the words he found. He was incredibly fluent in a

145

language I had never heard him use before, one I had never imagined he would know. It was the language of love.

'Sir John walked over to the one-way mirror and stared at you. Sir Max was transfixed – listening. By now the anger in the room had almost dissipated.

'Peter stopped talking and there was complete silence. The room was calm. Sir Max let out a long sigh. "So what are we going to do?" he said.

'Peter began to talk again. He told them that he believed you could be brought inside the Department. As he unfolded this idea to them, he acknowledged that they would have to take most of what he said about you on trust. However, he was prepared to test you in front of them right now. To demonstrate, so that they could see for themselves. He also gave them his word that if, after that, they were not satisfied, he would accept their decision – but on one condition. He himself would kill you. No-one else. He would do it.

'His belief in you stunned me, stunned them as well. They could do nothing but agree, so they told him to go ahead. Then they told him in some detail what he had to do. I listened, horrified, not believing for one moment that he would agree to do it, but he did. He never wavered.

'Peter left the room to change and prepare. I could think of nothing to say. I looked at you as you sat on your chair, patiently waiting for him. I understood that, because over the months I had seen how much you trusted him.

'I wondered: how was he going to explain to you what was happening, how was he going to prepare you for what he was about to do? It appeared an impossible task. Then I remembered the numerous times he had been given what appeared to be unachievable objectives and had succeeded with utmost brilliance. I knew that if anyone could save your life, it was Peter. I also knew that he believed he could do it. What I didn't know was why.

'I watched and waited, strangely fascinated by it all. It was about half an hour before Peter returned to the room. He asked me to switch on the camera. The camera recorded everything that happened in the room next door and had a red light to show that it was functioning.

'Turning to Sir Max, Peter said quietly, "Sir Max, when you and Sir John are satisfied, would you please switch off the camera. The red light will be a signal to me. If it has not gone out exactly two hours from when I enter the room, I will kill her."

'Sir Max and Sir John looked at each other and nodded. When Peter left the room, we drew three chairs up in front of the mirror and waited. The tension had returned and the room was very hot. I felt as if I was about to watch the final act of a real-life drama. I was.

'All I could do now was wait for the curtain to come up. The two men beside me looked uncomfortable and fidgeted continually. None of us could meet each other's eyes.

'Peter entered the room where you were and you stood up, sending the chair crashing behind you. I looked at my watch. The red light was clearly on in the room. "Christ!" I said under my breath. Time was already ticking away.

'I was shocked when he started telling you about the Department and his role in it. At that moment he sealed your fate. After he had revealed such information, there was no way back for you and he knew it. I thought he was gambling with your life and I couldn't believe it, but of course he knew you – we didn't.

'If I'm honest, Helen, at that moment I thought

147

you'd had it. I was appalled. I looked at the other two. They also realised what he had done – taken your life in his hands and thrown it into the ring. Sir John was gently shaking his head.

'Helen, I had been with Peter for almost ten years. I thought I knew him. The others thought they knew him even better. None of us were prepared for what happened that afternoon.

'We sat transfixed. Watching him with you was like watching someone work on an uncut diamond, administering clean, sharp, definite strokes until every facet of the diamond was revealed. It was as if he understood every nuance of your character, knew right down to the finest detail how to polish you, to bring out what he wanted to show us all – your brilliance, your light, your worth.

'When you fainted he caught you and lowered you ever so gently to the floor. I was amazed. He went to the door and called in two other men, giving them some brisk instructions.

'Twice Sir John signalled to Sir Max that he was satisfied. Twice Sir Max signalled back to wait. You were fighting to get up off the floor but it was obvious to all of us that you had no chance. The two men had been instructed not to let you. I could see you getting weaker but Peter's voice was the only spur you needed. You were determined to obey him.

'Then Sir Max's voice broke the silence in the room. "Neil, switch off the camera. Make sure that red light's extinguished now". I did it, and the light went off. Peter saw it but he continued watching you trying to get up with the help of the wall. The two men saw it and backed away from you. You were up with your back against the wall but swaying precariously. They fetched you a chair and sat you down, then they left. Peter didn't move. I was agog. We were all frozen. He wasn't finished. What did he want? I wondered. He just stood there watching you. You stood up.

'It was the work of a master. Not only had he proved to us that you could do it; he had gone beyond that, beyond their instructions. He had demanded more from you. No, that wasn't true. He had demanded nothing. He had known all along you would give it to him. He knew the diamond was top carat.

'When he came out of the room he looked exhausted. He gave me instructions to give to Paul back at his house and I left. When I got back to Belgravia I briefed Paul, then went to bed. I couldn't cope with any more.'

Neil paused. He looked at me and smiled. 'That was the day I realised he was deeply in love with you. That was the day he realised he was deeply in love with you. That was the day both of us realised what it meant. He has never discussed it with me, but it lies unsaid between us.'

# Chapter 16
# The Decision

After Neil had finished, I knew I would tell him.
'Peter has asked me to live with him here in
London,' I said.

Neil raised his eyebrows in obvious surprise – and
something else.

'But I can't,' I said quickly, sensing his anxiety.

Did I imagine it or did a quick look of relief pass
over his face?

'Why can't you?'

'The children. It's not suitable; it's not possible. I
can't do it. He doesn't really want them.'

Neil kept quiet and just looked at me, but I knew
what he was thinking.

'It's just not right anyway.' I hesitated.

'What's not right?' Neil asked quietly.

'It's not right for the children – I've explained that.
It's not right for Peter – it could destroy him, it could
destroy us. It's not right for the Department and he
knows that. It's not right for me because of all those
things. Oh, Neil – if I love him I must go. I must go
back and tell him.'

I realised there was a double meaning in what I
had just said. Yes, I had to go and tell him, but I also
had to go away.

'I must go back and tell him,' I repeated, trying to
deny the other reality that would not leave my head.

'I'll tell him for you, Helen, if you want.'

'No. Thank you, Neil, but I must tell him myself.'

He smiled. 'All right, we'll get a taxi and go back as
soon as you're ready.'

'Just give me a minute, Neil.'

I went to the cloakroom. I wanted to check my appearance, to eliminate any signs that I had been upset. Tears were okay with Peter, but not if he thought I was using them to try and influence him. Then he would have despised me. I also knew not to do anything by messenger. It was imperative that I told him myself, but I was frightened – frightened of his reaction, but most of all frightened of losing him.

When I returned Neil was talking to a man on the far side of the restaurant. From where I stood I could see he was good-looking in a rugged, outdoor sort of way. He was wearing a suit but he looked uncomfortable in it, and it looked even more uncomfortable on him. It didn't fit him properly: the sleeves were too short and the trousers too long. If he'd said it was borrowed from a friend, I would have believed him.

As I got closer I noticed deep-set, dark eyes, an outdoor complexion, a nose that had been broken several times and a scar above full, sensual lips. Neil said something that made him laugh, and the power and openness of his emotions were warming. As I approached he saw me and his eyes lit up questioningly.

Neil introduced us. 'Helen, meet another friend of mine, Stuart Hamilton. Stuart, this is Helen.'

We shook hands as I looked into a pair of twinkling, deepest blue-green eyes. After a few seconds' easy conversation Stuart excused himself and left.

I looked at Neil. 'Is he one of ours?' I said.

'No, not really. He's an officer in the Special Air Service.'

In the midst of all my unhappiness, somewhere in the back of my mind I registered the man's name. Then I forgot all about him.

Little did I know just how portentous that meeting was to be.

When we were safely in the taxi, I turned to Neil. 'How do you think Peter will react?'

'I don't know. This is a first for me and I suspect for him too. I've never known him to do anything like this before. Frankly, I'm very surprised.' I sensed the slight disapproval in his voice.

'I don't want to lose him, Neil, but I can't do this. I hope we can somehow just go on as we were before.'

Jessie's words came back to me – 'Relationships have to have a beginning, a middle and an end' – but I quickly dismissed them from my mind.

Neil patted my hand. 'I understand – let's hope that he does too.'

When we arrived at Peter's we walked up the steps together. Paul saw us coming and let us in. I asked Neil to tell Peter I was here and wanted to speak to him, then I put my things on one of the beautiful hand-carved chairs in the hall but stood waiting as Neil went upstairs. I heard him knock, then open the door. Almost immediately he called me.

'Helen. Come up please.'

I climbed the stairs, aware that the next few minutes could again change my whole life, just as it had changed years ago. Since that moment Peter had held my life in his hands and I could feel my heart pounding. Neil held the door open for me and I walked in. I heard him close it behind me; Peter and I were alone.

Why did so much of my life with this man depend on entrances and exits, like a stage play? But this was a real life drama and Peter and I were the principal players.

Peter was standing looking out of the window with his back to me. He was quite, quite still, but I noticed he kept flexing and unflexing the fingers of both his hands, which hung down by his side. After a few minutes silence I realised he was going to neither speak nor turn around.

I spoke quietly. 'Peter, I've come to tell you ...' I paused. 'I can't bring the children to London.'

'Then come without them.' His voice was icy.

'No, I'm not coming,' I said gently.

There was a long silence. Even the flexing of his fingers stopped. He was more than still; he was like a statue.

'Shall I go now?' I asked

'Yes,' came the immediate answer 'but before you do remember this.'

He turned and walked across the room. When he reached me I visibly stiffened. For a second I thought he was going to hit me. He took my hand and turned it until it was resting in his. 'Don't ever forget, Helen. I still hold you in the palm of my hand.' He dropped my hand and abruptly walked away. 'Now get out and this time don't come back.'

I moved towards him. I couldn't help myself. I wanted to reach out to him, to touch him. I could feel his pain but I couldn't get to it. As he heard me cross the room his voiced lashed out. 'Go! And go now!'

It was a voice I had never heard before. Shaking with emotion, it compelled obedience. I left the room. Neil was waiting outside the door. He looked shocked.

So I fled for the second time that day: down the stairs, through the hall, snatching my things off the chair. I left the front door wide open as I ran down the steps. I saw a taxi approaching, its lights denoting it was free. I hailed it and jumped in.

'Euston Station,' I said quickly.

I don't remember the journey home. I was in a state of shock. When I arrived I realised there was nothing to keep me there: the children were staying with my parents and Jessie was abroad. I had no-one I could confide in. I burst into tears as all the emotion

153

of the last few hours overwhelmed me. I walked around the garden, sobbing myself out, then came inside and made a cup of tea. After an hour I felt calm enough to know what I wanted to do and where I wanted to go. I made a phone call to check the children were okay and left a note by the phone to say where I was.

Then I got in my car and drove north. I knew exactly where I was going.

## Chapter 17
## Sharrow Bay

There were two places in England that I considered to be havens, refuges where I could go and be myself, where the people would not ask questions but would be sensitive to my situation.

One was the Savoy Hotel in London. I first went there with my father when I was about eight and at boarding school. At the end of term, girls could go by train to London, escorted by a teacher, as long as they were met there by a parent or guardian. My father would arrange business meetings in town so that on the day I broke up he could meet me at Waterloo Station.

Going to the Savoy with my father was one of those wonderful childhood experiences that have such a profound effect, they stay with you throughout your life. I still love the place today and I get the same feeling when I walk through the doors that I did as a child.

I can remember the joy when I saw my father on the platform and the warmth when he put his arms around me protectively. He would whisk me off in a taxi to the Savoy Hotel, where I would change out of my black school uniform into my best dress with white ankle socks and black patent bar shoes that my mother had carefully packed in his suitcase.

Then he would take me down to lunch in the restaurant overlooking the Thames – a little girl with the father she adored in such a beautiful place! Afterwards, he would usually take me to a matinee performance of one of the many musicals that were

155

playing in London at that time. A tired but blissfully happy child would then board a train home.

This happened many times and one particular day in the early nineteen fifties, we sat next to Sir Winston Churchill and his two sons-in-law, Christopher Soames and Duncan Sandys. Little did I know then how closely I would become involved in something so important to Churchill. He must have just been starting the Department with Peter at that time.

When he came into the restaurant, every man in the room stood up and bowed their heads in respect as he passed. It was very moving and even I, a little girl, was aware that I was in the presence of someone very special.

My father had briefed me about him before we went into lunch. He told me we were very honoured to have been put at the next table, and that I had to be very good. All the same, I could not resist saying in a very loud voice, 'Oh look, Daddy, look! He's having the steak, kidney and oyster pie with a whole bottle of red wine!'

My father chided me gently but Sir Winston looked across and smiled. 'No, no, child – pudding, pudding, not pie!'

'Daddy, daddy, daddy! He spoke to me!'

Fate had granted me the opportunity to meet him.

Now I was driving to my other refuge, Sharrow Bay Country House Hotel on Lake Ullswater in the Lake District. It was and still is undoubtedly one of the most wonderful hotels in the world.

There are so many things about it: its breathtakingly beautiful setting, nestling as it does at the far end of the lake; the ever-changing views; in the distance a mountain range with Striding Edge, a narrow ridge leading up to Helvelyn in the background.

Then there is the excellence of the hotel itself. I

could wax lyrical for hours, but let me just say it is faultless. I will leave you, the reader, to find out for yourself if you so wish.

But for me it was even more. It was a place where I could rest and renew my soul, where I could be alone and not feel lonely. A place that exuded warmth and sensitivity, somewhere I could go to that day, knowing I would find peace and the space to think.

I arrived late in the evening and was given a beautiful room overlooking the lake. I unpacked and had a long hot bath before going to bed and falling asleep almost immediately.

When I woke the next day I looked out of my window at the lake. It was raining softly and a mist hung over Helvelyn and the mountain range, so that only Hallin Fell opposite the hotel was visible. I spent the day gently walking beside the lake, breathing in the beauty. The rain had stopped and so had my tears, but not the immense pain. Now it turned colder and I hurried back to the hotel, grateful for the pot of tea brought to my room.

If you can think of somewhere, not someone, that you would go to if you were desperately unhappy, then you will understand what Sharrow Bay meant to me. I believe that David Jacobs, the television personality, went there to recover after his first wife was killed in a car accident. Other people I know have done the same.

The owners seemed to sense my emotional fragility without my having to say anything. They just surrounded me with unspoken empathy and spoilt me even more than usual. I had barely been there twenty-four hours but already I felt better, more in control of myself and my emotions.

Later that evening I contemplated trying to phone Peter, then thought better of it. Instead, I changed and went down to dinner. Soon after I retired to my room, there was a quiet tap on the door.

I opened it. There stood Jessie.

'Oh, darling!' I exclaimed, hearing the joy in my own voice. 'I'm so glad to see you! I thought you were in Florence.'

'I was. I came back early. I sensed you needed me. Your housekeeper told me where you were. Are you all right?'

'Yes ... no! ... Oh Jessie, I don't know. Come in ... come in.' I ushered her into the room and sat her down. 'Have you eaten? Do you want some coffee? Do want a drink, or anything?' The words tumbled out.

She laughed. 'Yes to the first, no to the other two. I'm fine, darling. I've arranged to stay here tonight. All I want is to know what's wrong.' She paused. 'It's Peter, isn't it?'

'Yes.' I sat down on the bed. Jessie waited patiently while I thought how to explain without telling her anything I shouldn't.

I looked across at her. As usual she was immaculate, every inch the lady. She was wearing the autumn colours she loved so much, a light tan pleated skirt with a cream silk blouse. Around the neckline she had folded a multicoloured silk scarf which I had given to her, orange, copper, sand and cream with the odd splash of lilac. A copper coloured jacket with matching shoes and handbag completed the outfit. I guessed she hadn't had time to change after her flight from Italy, but had come poste haste as soon as she knew where I was.

'Jessie – how do you stop loving someone?' I didn't wait for her to answer. 'He's asked me to live with him in London and I've said no.'

'Why?' she said gently. I said nothing. 'Is it because of the children?'

I hesitated, then: 'Yes, but it's not right for him either. He knows he can't commit himself like that, it's just not possible. Please don't ask me why, but it's not ... and now I think I've lost him.'

'Why?' she said again.

'He's angry and he's hurt and he told me to go away.' I stopped as I felt tears well up again and fought to hold them back.

Jessie waited, just watching me sympathetically. Then she said, 'Who is he angry with?'

'With me, of course.'

'Helen – are you sure? Perhaps, from what you've said, if he knows he can't do it he's angry with himself.' I looked at her, my mouth open. She continued. 'From what you've told me about him, he's a highly disciplined man who prides himself on the control he has over his life. I've been aware from what you've said that he's been fighting his love for you ever since he met you. Why, I don't know, but he must have a very good reason. That reason and his feelings for you are obviously in conflict, and he's angry. Unfortunately – too often for my liking – he takes it out on you.'

'Oh Jessie, it's partly my fault. I can't stop loving him and I can't let go – even though I know we can't be together.'

'Then you're both in the same bind.'

She was right, and she put it so clearly.

'You're so wise,' I said to her sadly.

'No, darling – just older. I understand because I've been in the same position. I loved someone but I knew it would never work. So did he.'

She explained it was one of the top Allied Commanders she had told me about. He had wanted to marry Jessie, but to do so he would have had to divorce his wife, which both he and Jessie knew would have been totally unacceptable to society at that time. He would almost certainly have lost his position and the respect of the whole world.

'What did you do?'

'We were lucky in that we both knew and had accepted it right from the start. But when we broke up it was still very painful.'

I remembered her tears the night we burnt the photographs and the letters.

'You and Peter didn't know, or didn't want to confront it,' she continued. 'You, Helen, went into flight mode and even I couldn't persuade you to look at your burgeoning love and consider where it was going. Peter went right into fight mode and tried to destroy his.'

That was true. I could not deny how hard Jessie had tried to warn me.

'What shall I do?' I almost whispered.

'Talk to him, reassure him. Explain that you understand what's happening. Then, if it is possible, enjoy what you have together. Enjoy it.' She smiled. 'Accept that you can't have more. Maybe it's a good thing this has happened. I knew something had to happen and I was afraid for you. Was he desperately cruel?'

'No, no, not really, just hurt and angry.'

Was that true? I wasn't sure. What had he meant when he said he still held me in the palm of his hand? Was it a threat or a simple statement of fact? Probably both, I thought.

And there was something else I had chosen not to look at. 'Do you think this is the end?' I blurted out, tears welling up again.

'Not necessarily, but I think you have to realise that this relationship carries a very high price. You both have to decide if it is a price worth paying.'

'What would you do, Jessie, if it was you?'

She looked out of the window at the lake, now bathed in moonlight, and I could see she was thinking. I didn't interrupt.

After a little while she turned and said slowly, 'I

would go to him – but not yet. I would give him time and space. Let the dust settle. When I did go to him I would make sure we were alone and there was no-one else around who would interrupt us. Don't make him feel manipulated, let him feel free to do and say as he pleases.

'Lastly, I would let him know I loved him, even at the risk of provoking his anger again. I believe, Helen, you will have to bring this to a head sometime. You can't run away from it forever.'

'Jessie, I ran because I didn't want to stay in case he said it was finished, and I don't want to hear that now.'

'Well, maybe he will say that, maybe he won't, but remember, darling – it's only when you turn round and run that you stumble and fall. You have to face him and sort it out together. Stop avoiding it and tell him to stop too.'

That made me grin. The idea of my lecturing Peter amused me.

'Helen, are you afraid of him?'

'Sometimes.'

'What are you afraid of?'

'Mainly the power – yet I love it too. I feel like a moth fascinated by the light – it's so bright, but when I get too close I get singed. Sometimes, I just want to run right into the middle of it all and damn the consequences.'

'What stops you doing that?'

'I'm not sure.' I struggled to find the answer. 'I want to – it's a bit like taking off a plaster when you're a child. If you try to pull it off gently, it hurts. You know it would be better to give one hard tug, which also hurts, but it's over quickly – do you know what I mean?'

'Go on,' she said.

'I know what you're saying, Jessie. I'm toying with

161

this thing with Peter, like a plaster, and being hurt anyway. I need to face it head on and get the pain over—'

Jessie interrupted me. 'Maybe you're not a moth attracted to the light but another light yourself that thinks it may be destroyed by one it perceives as more brilliant, so you veer away. That could happen, true, but maybe the two lights, if they joined together, would shine even brighter. You need to move in or move out – because moving around the edge is too dangerous, I think. It's burning into you. When your light dims, you move back, renew it and move forward again, but each time it's more damaging and ultimately it could destroy you.'

'Oh, Jessie!' I started to cry again.

'I'm sorry, Helen, but I love you and I know where you are. If you're in love with a man with that much personal power and you're caught in the turbulence of that power, short of running away there's only one thing to do. You must sail right into the eye of the storm.'

She got up and sat next to me, taking me in her arms as I cried calmly and quietly. I felt comforted and warm, knowing that she was there with me, understanding exactly how I felt.

'Come on, Helen,' she said gently, 'let's leave it there for now. We can talk again in the morning.'

Looking up, I saw how tired she was. Of course, she had flown back from Florence and then come straight here to help me.

'I'm being so selfish, Jessie. You must be tired out. I'm sorry. Let's go to bed.'

'Helen, I'm perfectly okay. Stop berating yourself. There's nowhere else I'd rather be than here with you and if I'm tired – well, it's a good tired and I shall sleep and be refreshed in the morning.'

She cupped my face gently with her hands and

kissed me on the forehead. 'Goodnight and God bless.'

I watched her walk out of the room and wondered once again how someone could be such a lovely person.

That night I slept fitfully, going over and over in my mind everything we had discussed. Yes, I had hoped Peter and I could go on as we were forever, but that was no longer possible.

When I said goodbye to Jessie the next day, I knew what I had to do. What I didn't know was how long it was going to be before I did it and what was going to happen in between.

## Chapter 18
## Geneva

Over the years I had learned to hide my feelings very successfully from my parents and they picked up very little. Occasionally my mother would sense something and ask if I was all right, but I would quickly reassure her and change the subject. I couldn't reveal what was going on in my life, and I didn't want to worry them. Anyway, I had never been able to confide in them about emotional issues: they belonged to the 'stiff-upper-lip' school which decreed that problems should be wallpapered over. If they did emerge, they had to be dealt with as quickly as possible and then forgotten.

Of course, my problem with Peter remained a running sore, something that couldn't be dealt with quickly, or forgotten.

In the weeks following my return from Sharrow Bay, I clung to the faint hope that Peter would contact me. I didn't want to believe he wouldn't, and I kept gazing wistfully at the phone, silently pleading: 'Ring! Please, please ring.'

I knew he wouldn't write to me. With him, nothing was ever put down in black and white. Even so, every morning I waited for the post, hoping there would be something, even just a coded message that I would understand. I was afraid to go out in case he called or came to the house and found me not there. My life revolved around the children and waiting for Peter to contact me.

But there was nothing.

After a month I realised it wasn't going to happen

and I was desolate. I felt utterly bereft. I'd been taken up into the stratosphere and then suddenly hurled back down, cut off from everything that had become dear to me. The loss was unimaginable.

As more months passed, I realised I had to get a grip of myself for the children's sake. I had to accept my return to Earth, even if it now felt totally alien to me. I made the most tremendous effort. Kidding myself that I was over Peter, I even started another relationship. The man was kind and caring and I made believe I loved him. He was wonderful with the children, he wanted to marry me.

My parents approved. Only Jessie cautioned me, advising restraint.

I didn't want to hear her. I convinced myself that this was the right thing to do. After all, the children would have a father now; we would be a family and all live happily ever after.

But, although I was back on Earth, I was lost, bumping around in the dark as if in a derailed ghost train. I was on the rebound, desperately needing someone and refusing to accept that it was Peter, that only he would do.

I married three months later.

I told my husband everything I could about Peter. He knew I was still in love with him but he married me anyway. I think he thought he could make me forget Peter, but he had set himself an impossible task.

I tried to be a good wife, a good mother, but underneath, every day I was dying a little. The truth wouldn't go away. I was still desperately in love with Peter. Now I knew what he had meant: he still held me in the palm of his hand. My husband knew it and so did I. Despite our bravest efforts, it was never going to work.

Eventually we accepted defeat and parted, not acrimoniously but with great sadness. We remained

HJH

good friends, even after his remarriage many years later, and I will always be grateful to him.

When we met, he had also been unhappy and he always said that we came together like a couple of kittens, lost and cold in the dark. We stayed together for warmth and comfort, and then we moved on. I think that was generous of him. He was a good man who believed he could make me forget Peter; it was not his fault that he couldn't.

Putting another tremendous strain on the relationship was my involvement in the Department, which was as unresolved as my feelings for Peter. Neither would ever let me go.

The one constant in my life through all of this was the children, who kept me grounded. I now know that they also kept me sane and enabled me to cope. They were my *raison d'être,* the fixed star in my life. Nothing and no-one could make me lose sight of that star.

Today I look at them with pride. They are well-adjusted, mature and successful adults. Over the years I was lucky to have the support of my parents and Jessie, all of whom the children adored, and because of that I was never afraid to leave them, although many times I was torn when Peter and the Department were too demanding.

Some time after my divorce, Jessie gently chided me. She knew how unhappy I was. 'Helen, it's time to stop running, darling.' I looked at her and saw the love in her face. 'It's time. You must bring this to a conclusion. Your life is on hold – there's so much unfinished business. You must go back before you can go forward – go to him.'

'But ... but.'

'No buts – you have nothing to lose with him that you don't feel you've lost already.'

166

I knew she was right but I was afraid. I had tried so hard to forget him, to get on with my life, but I had failed. Not only had I failed, but I had hurt a good man in the process.

I couldn't even get through one hour without Peter invading my thoughts: at home, at work, with the children. Even in my sleep my dreams were full of him.

Jessie was right. I had to go back, if only to bring things to a proper conclusion. At long last I knew – it was time to sail into the eye of the storm.

Nervously, I phoned London. Neil answered.

'Hello, Neil, it's Helen. Can you connect me to Peter?'

'He's in Geneva, Helen. He'll be there for another four days. I'm joining him this afternoon.' Then, almost as an afterthought, he added: 'He's at the Hotel Richemond.'

'Thanks, Neil – goodbye.' I hung up.

A sense of anticlimax hit me. I felt frustrated and disappointed. I phoned Jessie and told her what had happened.

'Do you know where he is in Geneva?' she asked.

'Oh yes.'

'Is your passport up to date?'

'Yes.'

'Then there's only one other question, isn't there?' She chuckled. 'I'll look after the children for you.' Then she was gone.

Of course, I thought, Geneva was perfect. I knew the city well. My father had sent me there for a year to learn French, and it was where I had met André. It also meant I would not have to beard the lion in his London den.

I arranged to fly out the following morning and spent the rest of the day in a flurry of activity, making sure I left everything Jessie would need to look after the children. She had clucked with pleasure when I told her I was going.

I arrived in Geneva at lunchtime. Jumping into a taxi, I practised my nearly forgotten French.

'Je voudrais aller à l'Hotel des Familles, s'il vous plaît. Il est près de la gare.'

'Ça va,' said the driver.

I knew the hotel. It was not luxurious, but it was comfortable. More important, it was within walking distance of the Hotel Richemond. I booked a room and then went in search of something to eat. I had refused food on the plane, but now Peter's training came to the fore and I knew I had to take some kind of nourishment. Soon I might need every bit of energy I could summon.

I went to a nearby cafe called Le Café Gare Centre and ordered *veau aux champignons*, a dish I had eaten there many times before. It was not a smart establishment and I was certain I would not see anyone from the Department there. I was not hungry but when my food came I ate the lot.

Checking my watch I saw it was now after three o'clock. I guessed if Peter was at meetings he wouldn't be back until five, but I decided it was time to go. I paid my bill and walked down towards the lake, where I watched the *jet d'eau*, its water surging upwards high above the city, then bending back to drop into Lake Leman.

Geneva was an ideal place for Peter to meet people from all over the world. It was an international city and of course, Switzerland, was a neutral country, safe and unaligned with the two then-superpowers – the United States and the Soviet Union.

Peter had a permanent suite on the sixth floor of

the Hotel Richemond. Although I still hadn't decided exactly what I was going to do, I thought I would try and wait for him there in the sitting room.

Soon I was at the entrance of the hotel. I went up the steps and walked in, praying that Peter would not be in the front hall. It was too public, and in a public place I knew he would be polite to me, however he felt. It would be awkward and false. I needed to see him alone.

I looked quickly around. Immediately I saw two men I recognised from the Department. Deciding that a show of confidence was the best thing, I walked up to them.

'Hello – is the Boss here?'

'No. He's not due back until about five.'

'Could you let me into the suite?' I said, then added, 'Please could you tell him I'm here when he comes back.'

That seemed to be enough. One of the men escorted me up to the suite and after unlocking the door he retreated back downstairs.

I walked through a hall and entered a room. I was in the sitting room of the suite. So far so good. I opened various doors. One led into a bedroom, another into a connecting bathroom. It was all beautifully appointed. In front of the window, looking across some gardens to the lake, was a coffee table and two comfortable chairs. On the table lay a book, *America*, by Alistair Cooke, whom I knew to be a friend of Peter's. I picked up the book and was not surprised to find he had autographed it.

I moved on. There was a drinks cabinet against one wall. On the opposite wall was a bookcase and beside the entrance door, a gramophone. I walked over and lifted the lid. There was a record on the turntable; without looking to see what it was, I switched on the power and pressed PLAY.

To me, the music was instantly recognisable. It was Max Bruchs' Violin Concerto and I was almost certain the violin was played by Igor Oistrakh. It was one of Peter's favourite pieces and we had listened to it many times together. I sat down and waited. The intense yearning of the music filled the room and, maybe unwisely, I let it invade my soul.

When the record finished, I sat quite still. I felt very nervous and it occurred to me that the last time I had sat like this in a room, waiting for Peter to appear, was the day in London when I broke his cover. Oh, I had changed since then, but in some respects I was still the same girl who felt the same fear.

Looking out of the windows, I saw three men in the distance walking alongside the lake. Although they were too far away for me to make out their features, I knew immediately that the one in the centre was Peter. It was just the way he carried himself, his walk. As they came nearer, through the gardens, I saw Neil on one side of him and a man I didn't recognise on the other.

Peter looked wonderful. He was wearing a suit but had taken off the jacket and was swinging it casually in one hand over his shoulder. He looked fit and tanned and was laughing with the man I didn't recognise. I felt myself choke up inside.

They reached the hotel entrance below and disappeared inside. I stood up quickly and took some deep breaths. Oh God, I thought. What am I doing here? At that moment I wished I hadn't come.

I checked my watch. It was nearly five o'clock. I waited. Five minutes went by, then ten, then fifteen. I felt even more nervous. I was sure the men downstairs would have told Peter immediately that I was here. Should I go down? No. He might think I was running away. I sat down again.

At that very moment the door opened and Peter walked in, followed by Neil.

I stood up. His face gave nothing away.

'Helen,' he said, 'I've booked you on the eight-thirty flight to London. Neil will take you to the airport now. You will be on that flight. Do you understand?'

Before I could say anything, he walked across the room, into the bedroom and shut the door. I looked at Neil, who shrugged and gave me a sort of smile.

'What happened downstairs?' I whispered miserably.

'Come on. I'll tell you on the way to the airport. Have you got any luggage?'

I explained it was at the other hotel; we could pick it up on the way. I turned towards the bedroom door and stared at it. Neil saw me.

'No! No, Helen, don't you even think about it. Not at the moment. He has another crucial meeting in about ten minutes. Come on – I'll talk to you when we're away from here.'

I saw the anxiety on his face and did not argue. Picking up my handbag I walked to the door. Then I stopped and, on impulse, went over to the gramophone, put the record back on and turned up the sound.

Neil calmly turned it down. 'It's okay,' he said, 'it's piped through to the bedroom.'

We didn't talk much in the taxi but when we arrived at the airport Neil found a quiet area and we sat down. I said nothing, just looked at him. He started talking.

'When we arrived back at the hotel they told him you were there. I don't know what he thought. He just paused. After a few moments he instructed me to book you onto the next flight to London – nothing else. I think you were very unlucky. This next meeting he has tonight is the final one but the most crucial. I

171

don't think he could afford to take his eye off the ball.'

'Is this meeting in his suite at the Richemond?' I asked.

'Yes.'

'Oh, I see.'

I was very quiet, trying to think what to do. I was damned if I was going to be sent back to London like a naughty child. Not after all this. I turned to Neil.

'Thank you, Neil. I know how you feel about Peter and me, and I understand. I know we can never live together, but we can't just end it like this. There's too much between us, so much unfinished business. Unless I have the chance to talk to him, to get through to him, we can't sort it out.' I paused. 'How has he been since I last saw him?'

'Closed down – completely closed down.'

'Not completely, Neil. Did you hear that music? It's one of the most emotional pieces ever written. I defy anyone to say that someone who chooses to listen to that particular music is closed down. I think he's hurting as much as I am.'

'Yes, Helen, but I've known him many years and the way he handles these situations is to bring down a steel shutter between him and whatever it is.'

'Yes and somehow I have to reach him. Only that way will he lift it,' I said.

'You're incredibly stubborn, aren't you?'

'Yes – it's one of my greatest failings. I can't let go. But Neil, you said yourself I'm good for him and I understand now what we can and can't have. Most important, I really love him and I believe he loves me. Why shouldn't I fight?'

He smiled. 'There's nothing I can say to that, is there?'

We sat together in silence. We were both thinking and there was an easy camaraderie between us. I knew this man also loved Peter and that, despite the problems, he liked me too. So I felt at ease with him and I trusted him, as much as I now trusted anyone.

'Neil,' I said, suddenly sure. 'I'm not going on this flight. I'm going back to the Hotel des Familles. Will you do something for me? Will you phone me there when he's finished his meeting? Oh – and of course I realise you won't lie if he asks you any questions.'

'He'll probably only ask me if I took you to the airport.'

'Yes – well that's exactly what you did.'

He grinned and shook his head. 'Helen, I wish you luck. I won't ask you what you're going to do after I phone you.' He stood up.

'I couldn't tell you if you did, Neil. You see, I haven't decided yet. After all, wasn't it the Boss himself who taught us to keep all options open until we really have to make a decision?'

I walked to the entrance with him. 'Bye for now and thank you again.'

He smiled and walked away.

I took a taxi back to the hotel and checked in again. They looked at me rather strangely, but made no comment. They probably just thought I was another eccentric *Anglaise*. I didn't care anyway.

I went to my room and waited. At half past nine the phone rang. It was Neil. 'They've left.'

'Is he alone?'

'Yes – and he's dismissed us for the night.'

'Did he say anything?'

'He asked if I'd taken you to the airport and I said yes. That was all.'

'Thank you, Neil – goodnight.'

'Goodnight, Helen.'

I replaced the receiver but picked it up again immediately and phoned the Richemond. I asked them to connect me to Peter's suite. I could hear it ringing.

173

'Hello.' It was Peter.

'Hello,' I said quietly, 'I need to ask you something.'
Silence. 'I can't ask you on the phone. Please may I
come over?'

'Where are you?' Very controlled.

'Hotel des Familles.'

There was a long, long silence. Eventually he spoke.
'I'll come to you. What's your room number?'

'One hundred and twenty.'

*Click.* The line went dead.

Twenty minutes later, my door opened and in
walked Peter. This time he was alone. He shut the
door and turned to face me.

'Take off your clothes and get on the bed. After all,
that's what you've come for, isn't it?'

I was astounded. Whatever else I might have
expected, it wasn't that. He had thrown me completely.
I could think of nothing to say. All I was sure of at
that moment was that I was not going to do what he
said.

'Are you going to disobey me again?'

I was speechless, frozen in shock.

'Take your clothes off now, or I'll do it for you.'

He approached me and deliberately began to undo
the top button of my blouse. My hand came out as if
from nowhere and I slapped him hard across the face.
The noise as I hit him sounded like the crack of a
whip. I was horrified.

He stood there and looked at me. The silence went
on and on. I could not speak. His eyes were relentless,
my finger marks red across his cheek. I shook my head
and slumped down onto the bed. What had I done?

He continued to stare at me. Now what would he
do? Now I was in real trouble, and with nowhere to
go.

Abruptly he turned, took my jacket off the back of
the door and threw it at me.

'Put that on – we're going out.'

I was lost and he knew it. I was really frightened, and I felt so weak. All my emotional and physical energy had dissipated with that slap.

Now he truly held me in the palm of his hand.

I followed him: down the stairs, past the receptionist and out into the night. He walked, blank and silent. Any emotion from him would have been easier to handle but there was nothing. He wasn't even cold – just utterly impassive.

It was this impassivity that was so frightening, more frightening than anything I had experienced with him before. I wondered if this time he was going to kill me. That way for sure he could remove forever the threat of our love.

We turned left and went down some steps. I could hear music. My mind was racing ahead. Would this drown out any noise as he murdered me? Would I be found the next morning dead in some back alley in Geneva?

Yet I still followed as if pulled along by a rope. I didn't dare disobey him. At that moment I hadn't the strength, never mind the courage.

At the bottom of the steps, he opened a door on his right and signalled me to go in first. The music was now much louder and when I stepped inside I realised I was in a nightclub. Someone came up and took my jacket, then ushered us to a table. I sat down and Peter ordered some wine. He still didn't speak to me.

As soon as the wine came he stood up, grasped my arm and walked me onto the dance floor. He started to dance. It was not the kind of dancing where you held each other, but modern dance, so I was disconnected from him and yet with him. I had to follow him.

The music was unrelenting and so was he. He

danced with immense energy and intensity, never looking at me, never connecting with me, but I was forced to keep in step with him. I was totally in his control.

After an hour I was tired. 'Please can we stop?' I said.

He didn't answer, and I thought perhaps he hadn't heard me.

'Please can we stop?' I said louder.

He grabbed my arm. 'Dance!'

We must have danced for over two hours. I was exhausted and I could see beads of sweat on Peter's forehead. I knew I could not go on much longer, but I was too afraid to stop, too drained to think. I was an automaton.

Then luck intervened: the music stopped as the band took a break. Peter grasped me by my arm again and we left. He half carried me back to the hotel, up the stairs and into my room. He threw me down onto the only armchair, picked up the luggage rack, put it right up against my legs, then sat astride it in an interrogatory position.

I felt utterly vulnerable, trapped by him and the luggage rack.

'Now – what was the question you wanted to ask me?' His voice was colder than ice.

I hesitated, then very quietly I said, 'How do I stop loving you?'

His eyes narrowed. He stood up and walked over to the door. I thought he was going to leave. Then he turned round. 'I'll answer that question in the morning. Goodnight.'

And he left.

I waited until I heard his footsteps disappear down the stairs. Then I burst into tears. I pushed the luggage rack away from the chair so that I could get up, and stumbled into the bathroom.

Looking in the mirror I saw that I was dishevelled; my hair hung in tendrils, mascara smeared my cheeks. I turned on the shower, let the water beat down on me, then I dried myself and went to bed, where I began to relax. Perhaps now the worst was over.

How wrong could a person be.

# Chapter 19
# The Morning After

I awoke sometime during the night and for a moment I thought the whole thing had been a dream. When the realisation dawned that it hadn't, I could not go back to sleep and lay awake thinking about everything that had happened.

It had not surprised me that Peter had given priority to a crucial Department meeting, refusing to see me until it was over. Had it not been for that, I don't think he would have refused, whatever his feelings on discovering I was in Geneva; it was not his style. Nor had it surprised me that he was angry with me for not taking the flight back to London as he had instructed.

But nothing had prepared me for what he had said when he came to my hotel room, or for my own loss of self-control. I still couldn't believe I had hit him. I must have taken him by surprise as much as myself, otherwise I would never have been able to make physical contact; he was far too highly trained.

As I lay there, I trembled when I thought about it. I realised just how vulnerable I had made myself. He could have ripped my clothes off and forcibly taken me. After all, he had done it before. But he didn't.

He could have physically demolished me. But he chose not to. Instead he had used the dancing to channel his anger and emotions.

I knew I was very lucky.

As usual where Peter was concerned, the whole thing had centred around control. He had taught me a great deal about that but he also knew how to break down the very control he had fostered, and he had succeeded so easily.

Too easily for him to leave it, which I was to find out shortly.

As long as Peter saw our situation as some kind of battle, he would certainly win. Somehow I had to make him understand I was not fighting him, that I would not fight him – but how, without losing my self-respect and thereby losing his?

For me, the bottom line was about being true to myself. I would hold onto that for grim death and see what happened next. After all, Peter had said he would answer my question in the morning so at least I had one more chance.

How could I show him that I wanted us both to win? How could I persuade him to let me in behind that awesome control he demanded of himself and all of us? And had I any right to?

If I damaged or threatened that control, then I damaged the Department and that was unacceptable. Could I find a place for us that didn't threaten either?

I didn't know, but I did know I was damn well going to try – because I also knew with absolute clarity that Peter needed me to retain his humanity, his ability to feel, maybe his very sanity. However ridiculous it may sound, I was afraid for him  This man was extraordinary, but he carried too much. His work was so important, not just for Great Britain but for the world. I knew how much he was doing, how much influence he had on men who were responsible for decisions that affected millions of people. They respected him, listened to him and trusted him. They needed him.

His country asked too much of him and he would never say no. He also demanded too much of himself and there were times when he was tested to the limit. These were the times that made me forgive his cruelty and thoughtlessness towards me. I understood, because for him there were so few resting-places.

I knew when he did come to rest, it was to me. I was his harbour.

One question I didn't ask myself in those early hours was how Peter had felt when he left me the night before. I just assumed he must be furious with me. But if Jessie had been there she would have said, 'How do you know he's angry? Who is he angry with? What is he angry about?'

At eight o'clock the phone rang. It was Neil.

'Helen, come over to the Richemond at ten. I'll meet you downstairs.'

I agreed, and after a quick shower I chose a pretty blue and yellow cotton dress, simple but very feminine. I went downstairs and although I didn't feel hungry, I went to the same cafe as the day before and ordered a café complet.

It was a lovely Saturday and after my coffee I decided to go down to the lake and walk around the gardens. Parents were out with their children and I was struck by how beautifully the children were dressed, and what a wealthy city Geneva was.

At exactly five to ten I walked into the Hotel Richemond. Neil was there in the foyer and he signalled me to come over and sit with him.

He smiled. 'You look lovely.'

'Thank you,' I said, my hopes rising. But the smile disappeared.

'If you want to see him you can, but you are to be on parade. He's given you no choice.'

I stared at him. 'But Neil, that will make it almost impossible to talk to him.'

He ignored my comment. 'What happened last night?'

I hesitated. Could I tell him? No, it was too

personal. 'I don't think I can tell you, but why do you ask? Help me, Neil.'

He frowned. 'I'm not sure I can.'

There was silence, then I heard myself say quietly, 'I refused to do something. He tried to make me and I hit him.'

'You what?' Neil was horrified.

'I slapped him across the face,' I said, almost in a whisper.

'Oh my God, Helen. What did he do?'

'Nothing.' Now I was whispering. 'He took me dancing.'

'He *what?*'

'He took me dancing.'

'And then what?'

'He took me home.'

Neil shook his head. I could see he was perplexed. 'Didn't he say anything?'

'No, except when we got back to the hotel. I asked him a question and he said he would answer it today.'

'What was the question?'

'How could I stop loving him?'

'Oh Christ, Helen.'

'What's the matter?'

He shook his head again. 'You're walking right into it. He's put you on parade and if you see him he can do anything he wants.'

'Neil,' I said quietly, 'he can anyway.'

'Yes but this way you have to obey him.'

'Yes, that's right.'

I felt suddenly calm. At that moment I saw it – a possible way through the storm to the eye that Jessie had spoken of. I wasn't quite sure what I would find when I got there, but at least I now saw a way through.

'It's okay, Neil, I'm going to see him.' Standing up, I smiled at him and continued, 'Thank you, you've helped me more than you can ever know.'

181

'Helen – be careful.'

'I will.'

I walked away across the hall and up the stairs. I had no idea what was going to happen but at least I knew now what I had to do. As long as I was on parade and in control, I would retain not only my own respect but his as well.

By putting me on parade he had set me free.

Outside the door of the suite I knocked immediately.

'Come in.'

I entered. Peter was standing at the window. 'Good morning Helen.'

'Good morning, sir.'

I walked to the middle of the room and stood waiting. As he spoke he turned away and looked out of the window.

'Go into the bedroom. Remove your clothes and lie on the bed.'

Slowly I walked towards the bedroom door.

'Stop.' His voice rang across the room and I turned. 'What are you doing?'

'I'm obeying an order, sir.'

'And if it were not an order?'

'Then I would die rather than do it, sir.'

He frowned. 'Repeat the question you asked me last night.'

'How do I stop loving you, sir?'

He walked towards me. 'Maybe I can stop you, Helen.'

He opened the bedroom door. I walked through.

'Wait!' he commanded. He went over to the door that led to the corridor and opened it. Two men came in and stood staring at me. Their whole demeanour was threatening.

Peter turned to me. 'Now obey me. Take off your clothes and lie on the bed.'

That was the moment.

I just stood there. I knew this was it: I was right in the eye of the storm. There was nothing to do but wait. I could only do what this man in front of me had taught me to do.

This time I would get it right. I would stay in control of myself, even though I had no control over anything else. He would do what he wished. I could not stop him, but I would not take off my clothes. I would not lie on the bed. I would not obey him. If this time he came to undress me, then so be it.

I would stay true to myself.

At last I understood what he meant by control. Peter could do whatever he wanted to me. There was no way I could physically stop him, just as we cannot control the world around us. The only control we can have is over ourselves – and that is the most valuable of all.

The inner calm remained; in fact it grew. I felt strangely at peace, as if I had come home. The silence went on and on but it didn't worry me. I was at the epicentre and now I understood that the epicentre was in myself. It was not dependent on anyone or anything else.

Peter walked round and behind me. I stayed quite still. I heard a door shut. I didn't move. None of it mattered.

He came back in front of me and he smiled. It was a gentle smile.

He guided me into the sitting room and, sitting me down, started to ask me questions.

'What do you think I was doing last night?'

'I thought then that you were trying to humiliate me, sir. Now I know different.'

'Yes ... but what made you think I might want to do that?'

'Maybe so that I wouldn't love you any more, sir.'

'Why would I not want you to love me any more?'

For a second I wanted to duck the question but I didn't. 'Because you're afraid, sir,' I said very quietly.

He raised an eyebrow. 'What am I afraid of?' he said with a quizzical look on his face.

'Your feelings for me, sir.'

'How do you know what I feel about you?' His face was expressionless again.

'I just do, sir.'

'Oh I see. So, how do I feel about you?'

'You love me, sir.'

'If I love you as you say, why should I be afraid of you?'

'I think, sir, you're afraid of your love for me – not me.'

The eyebrow went up again. 'I think you're right. Now tell me why I should be afraid of loving you.'

I paused and wondered where to start. My answer was going to be crucial. I knew what he was doing: he was making me answer the questions he could not or did not want to answer himself. It was another of his strengths: when he didn't have the answer he would draw on other people's knowledge without losing any authority himself. In matters of love, he was in unknown territory.

I looked up into the corner of the room. 'Sir, will you give me a moment. I want to get this right.'

He was silent. The minutes ticked by but he said nothing. Gradually my thoughts came into line.

'Firstly and above all else, sir, you believe it would damage the Department. It is against your own rules. It is unknown territory for you. I have a feeling,' I said even more quietly, 'that you have never been in love before. I also feel, though I may be wrong, that your whole life, even as a small child, has been loveless.'

I hesitated before speaking again. 'If that's true, sir, then if it were me, I would be terrified too.'

There was complete silence. I didn't dare move. I waited. Peter got up, walked over to the windows and stood with his back to me. I noticed he was clenching and unclenching his fists, always a sign that he was fighting for some sort of control, either mental or physical.

I stayed absolutely still. All I could hear was the hum of the air conditioning and the traffic in the street below. There was a *ding* as the lift in the corridor reached our floor, then the silence continued for well over five minutes. I knew well enough not to break it.

I suspected that Peter was overcome with emotion, and although every part of me wanted to rush over and comfort him, my instincts told me to leave him alone.

Time became suspended. I waited, and finally I saw his fists stop clenching. He appeared to be staring out over the lake. Quietly, I crossed the room to the door, opened it and went out. As I turned to close it I saw that he had not moved.

I was conscious that I was still on parade and that I had not been dismissed. I did not plan to go far but I left out of respect for him, because I knew I had touched something very deep and had no right to invade any further.

As I reached the hall I saw Neil.

'If the boss wants me I'm in the Brunswick Gardens just across from the hotel,' I told him.

He looked concerned, so I squeezed his arm gently. 'Leave him – he's okay.'

I walked across the road and sat down in the gardens under the statue, still feeling at peace. Somehow I knew that everything was all right. I lifted my face to the sun as it beat gently down on me. The breeze from the lake was just enough to lift the flags flying from the top of the garden café, and I let my thoughts drift with it.

They were rudely interrupted by the sound of a car horn. It was persistent so I turned to look and there, sitting in an open-top Cabriolet, was Peter, looking as if he hadn't a care in the world. There was a broad grin across his elegant features and an emerald green cashmere sweater was tied casually round his shoulders.

'Get in, Helen,' he called, 'we're going out to lunch.'

I flew across the road and into the car, my smile as broad as his. I saw Neil standing at the entrance of the hotel and waved gaily to him. He grinned and waved back.

'Have you got your passport?' Peter asked.

'Yes, sir,' I said, conscious that I was still on parade.

'Good – you can drop the "sir" now, we're off parade.'

He turned back to the wheel and started to drive the car through Geneva. Soon we were out in the countryside. He slowed down and visibly relaxed, taking one hand off the wheel and putting it across the back of my seat.

'Where are we going?' I asked, my curiosity as usual overwhelming my earlier decision to keep quiet.

'Talloires – a little place near Annecy in France.' He grinned like a young boy. His happiness was infectious and I caught it, bouncing up and down on my seat with excitement like the little girl I had once been.

I knew that we were going to have one of those wonderful days together and my spirits soared. When Peter was like this, nothing could compare to him. Perhaps as a result of his single-mindedness, which was normally devoted to the Department, he knew how to make you feel as if you were the only thing in the world that mattered. It was still such a rare occurrence that when it happened, I savoured every second.

We reached the Swiss/French border and Peter waved the two passports at the *gendarmes*. They picked up our happiness and laughingly waved us through, shouting, 'Allez-en, allez-en!'

We drove slowly through the countryside. The Mont Blanc mountain range stood out, and although it was summer, the tips of the mountains were still covered with snow. It was such a clear day we could see the top of Mont Blanc itself. The mountains contrasted starkly with the valley we were driving through, which was green and lush with flowers.

We didn't talk much; we didn't need to. I knew that would come later, when he was ready. For now, being with him was enough. Knowing he was happy released me and allowed me to feel the same.

We arrived at Annecy and drove along the lake, through various villages until Peter turned the car sharply right and we began to drop down towards the edge of the lake into the village of Tailloires.

'There it is,' he said, and I saw the sign 'Auberge du Père Bise' above the entrance to a cosy-looking inn. He drove the car into the drive and parked.

Peter walked in ahead of me, through the building and outside to a garden restaurant with a terrace overlooking Lake d'Annecy. Tables were dotted between shady trees and parasols, and the view over the lake was beautiful. It was an exquisite setting.

The maitre d'hotel came forward and greeted Peter as an old friend before ushering us to a quiet table. As soon as we were seated a waiter approached.

'Bonjour, Monsieur Peter. Comment allez-vous?'

Peter replied in fluent French. 'Hello, Claud, I'm fine. How are you?'

'I'm very well, Monsieur.' He paused and looked at me. 'The lady is very, very beautiful' – I smiled – 'and charming too.'

The French, I thought, are always so obvious.

187

I sat back in my chair and allowed myself to savour the whole scene while Claud went to an ice bucket under a tree and returned with a bottle of champagne. It had a black label so I realised it was Dom Perignon, Peter's favourite. With consummate ease Claud levered off the cork and exclaimed with delight at the loud pop, then he poured a small quantity into Peter's glass. At his nod of approval, Claud half-filled both glasses, then discreetly withdrew.

Peter raised his glass to me and smiled. 'Here's to love,' he said.

We touched glasses. The world around seemed to anticipate our need for privacy and moved back. There was only us.

'I love you, Helen.'

I smiled wistfully at him and said quietly, 'I know you do.'

'How long have you known?'

'I've known since the day I broke your cover.'

'I've known since then too.'

'What are we going to do?'

'What do you want to do?'

'I don't care,' I said recklessly, 'as long as I can be with you as often as possible. I love you so much.'

He nodded and took my hand, gently turning it over and tracing the scar from the cigarette burn with his index finger. Then he lifted my hand to his lips and tenderly kissed the scar.

This was the Peter that no-one else ever saw, the man I selfishly wanted to have with me all the time. I wondered now if that would ever be possible.

In front of his team, in front of the others, I knew he would have to be as hard and as ruthless as he had always been. But from that day, I hoped that when the door shut and we were on our own, he could be this Peter: the Peter I had so rarely seen in the preceding years.

Claud came back and Peter told him we would have the menu. I was happy to let him take charge. When the meal came it was superb, and complemented our mood. Like instruments in an orchestra, each dish came in at just the right moment and completed the symphony of happiness.

As is usual in France, we took our time over the meal. The French believe one must savour the whole experience, and we certainly did. When I eventually glanced at my watch, it was nearly five o'clock but neither of us was concerned.

Peter now turned the conversation round.

'I have been asking you all the questions, Helen. What do you want to ask me?'

'Can I ask you anything?'

He grinned. 'You can ask,' he said pointedly.

'Were you angry with me for coming to Geneva?'

'No, not at all.'

'Were you angry when I refused to do what you said last night?'

'No, I didn't think you would, and I certainly hoped you wouldn't.'

'Were you angry when I hit you?'

He paused and then smiled. 'Surprised. If I was angry it was with myself for underestimating you and allowing you to get the blow in.'

'Have you been angry with me at all over the last twenty-four hours?'

'No.'

I looked at him, puzzled. I was trying to understand.

'You don't understand, do you, Helen?'

'No,' I said plaintively. This time he took both my hands in his across the table.

'Everything you said this morning was true. Not only have I wanted to destroy our love, but there have been times when I wanted to destroy you too.'

I looked quickly down at the table. He stroked my hands gently but said no more.

'Do you still want to?' I asked, looking up suddenly, the words tumbling out before I could stop them. The minute I asked I wished I could take the question back.

He didn't answer. The question hung in the air between us. After a while I looked at him and said, 'It doesn't matter. I love you enough to live without an answer to that.'

Now it was his turn to look away.

'I'll pay the bill,' he said suddenly. 'Stay here. I'll be back in a minute.'

His voice was gentle and I knew that everything was still okay. Five minutes later he was back.

'Come on,' he said. Taking my arm he guided me to the car. The sun had gone down and he had put the hood up. We drove back to Geneva in comfortable silence, the kind of silence that can only envelope two people who are totally at ease with each other. I rested my hand gently on his thigh and from time to time he looked across and smiled at me.

When we arrived at the Richemond we went straight to his suite. He spoke briefly on the phone and dismissed his aides for the night. I noticed that my luggage had already been brought across from the Hotel des Familles.

I will draw a veil over the rest of the evening and leave it in the imagination of my reader.

The time we spent at Talloires was the first of three days that were the most magical of my life so far. I went through a door and reached a depth of feeling within myself that I barely knew existed. It was something that had been stirred in me occasionally by certain pieces of music, or the beauty of nature, a work of art or dance, but never like this, and never by another human being.

## Chapter 20
## The Aftermath

When I woke the next morning, Peter was already up. 'Good morning, sleepyhead,' he smiled at me. 'Would you like to go to the mountains today?'

'Oh I'd love to, but I don't have anything suitable to wear.'

'That's no problem. You wait here.' He grinned and was gone.

I stretched out on the bed and contemplated the world. At that moment it was a lovely place. If only it could always be like this. Then Jessie's words came into my mind. *Enjoy what you have.*

She was right. I bounced out of bed, went to the bathroom and had a long soak. Then I wrapped myself in a towelling dressing gown and went to relax in the sitting room. There was a knock at the door.

'Entrez,' I called, and in walked a waiter carrying a tray. It contained Swiss *ballons*, hot croissants, butter, cheese and confectionery, plus two large pots of coffee. It all smelt delicious and I was ravenously hungry, so I tucked in.

About twenty minutes later the door opened and Peter walked in. He wore a broad grin but said nothing, just sat down on the other chair and helped himself to breakfast.

Shortly there was another knock at the door.

'Entrez!' called Peter, and a man came in with three boxes. Peter told him where to put them, gave him a tip and, after the man had gone, turned to me and said, 'Those, beautiful girl, are for you.'

191

I crossed the room and started opening the parcels. Inside the first was a pair of walking shoes and some socks.

'Put them on,' he said. I did and they fitted perfectly.

Inside the second box were a pair of navy blue slacks, a cream silk blouse and a pale blue cardigan embroidered around the collar and cuffs with alpine flowers. In the last box was a very plain navy blue suede jacket.

'Put them on, put them on,' Peter insisted. I giggled and did as he said. Everything fitted perfectly. The clothes were beautiful and I twirled around excitedly, posing in front of him.

'They're so lovely! How did you know my size? You shouldn't have. Oh, thank you!'

He threw his head back and roared with laughter.

Peter had given me presents before. The first time he had thrown a carrier bag at me, saying, 'That's for you.' Inside had been an exquisite red dress which fitted me like a glove. The second time it was a beautiful emerald green cashmere coat. They were both chosen personally by Peter. He knew exactly what would suit me, right down to the subtlest shade of colour.

This would have been unusual in any man, but in Peter it seemed completely out of character. It was another example of the contrasts in him which made him so remarkable and so difficult to predict.

This pulled me even closer towards him. It wasn't the gift, it was the sudden sensitivity and thoughtfulness that I would never have anticipated. That, combined with the obvious pleasure he derived from giving, was irresistible, especially when placed beside his usual coldness and control.

Suddenly, a thought came into my head. For some reason I didn't understand, I felt that there might be a connection between him doing things like this and his desire to destroy me. Perhaps when he had been uncharacteristically warm and kind, he felt a need to be cold and cruel to the same degree. That way he could maintain the incredible control over himself which was so vital.

Why hadn't I pushed him to answer my question, 'Do you still want to destroy me?' Should I ask him again?

It dawned on me that perhaps I didn't want to know. Oh God! I was flirting with danger again and I knew it was very unwise, but it was utterly intoxicating. I thought I had mastered this urge – obviously not. I quickly tried to close down on the thought but not quickly enough. Peter had noticed.

'What are you thinking?' he said.

I foolishly tried to avoid the question, but I should have known better.

'It's Sunday – the shops are closed. How did you do this?' I murmured, stroking the softness of his jacket.

'I know the owner of a shop nearby so I just asked him to open it for me.'

'Did you choose them all yourself?'

'Yes. Now, Helen, tell me, what you were thinking back there?'

I gazed at Peter. It was pointless to try and avoid the question again, and I wasn't going to lie to him.

'I was thinking that I still like flirting with danger.'

'Why didn't you want to tell me?'

There was a silence. I looked away, struggling to find an acceptable answer that was also the truth.

'Because you're dangerous and I wanted to play with that.'

'How dangerous do you think I am?'

I could see he had no intention of letting me off the hook. I thought he might have laughed at that response. As it was, I was getting in deeper every second. The proverb 'when in hole, stop digging' applied to me at that moment. Of course I didn't, although I saw all the warning signals.

'As dangerous as you have to be.'

His response came back without so much as a pause. 'And how dangerous do I have to be?'

I gave up at that point and said, 'I don't know.'

'Well, think about it.' He walked out of the room.

I didn't have to; I knew what I had done. Oh damn, I thought. Would I ever be able to control this need to play with fire?

When Peter came back he was carrying a picnic basket and had a lightweight jacket over his arm. He smiled.

'Did you work it out?'

'Yes,' I said.

In just a few unguarded moments he had exposed my particular vulnerability. I knew why he had done it: it was absolutely necessary for those with him to be aware of any potential weaknesses so that they could guard against them. He knew mine was still present in me and he was always trying to help me get a grip of it, though I never did entirely.

We drove out and up into the mountains. We walked in the sun and picked the delicate alpine flowers. Peter threaded one into a necklace like a daisy chain and hung it round my neck. We played like a couple of children. It was hard to believe we were not in a dream.

He produced the picnic basket and a rug from the boot of the car, and we whiled away the afternoon. The Department did not exist up there in the mountains. Peter was totally relaxed – the man I guess he could have been were it not for the Department.

As the evening closed in and the sun began to go down behind the mountains, I sensed a sadness come over him. I went up to him and put my arms around him tentatively, something I had never done before. Some instinct had always guided me to wait for him to take the initiative, but since Talloires, when he had spoken to me in depth about his loveless childhood, I understood. If you have never received spontaneous affection, it is difficult to accept. For a second he hesitated, then he took me in his arms and we held each other.

'We have to go back,' he said.

'I know – but now, we have this.'

'Do we?' he asked cynically.

'No one can take it away. What we have at this moment is ours.'

'I wish I had your faith.'

The cynicism gave an edge to his voice. 'Tomorrow I have to be back in London. Tomorrow I'm responsible for the Department with everything that entails.'

'I know – but—'

He stopped me. 'There can't be any buts. It has to be all or nothing. I knew that when I started.'

I pulled back from his arms so that I could look at him. 'If you want me to go away again, I will.'

He paused. 'This morning before we left I spoke to Sir Max. I'm being called upon to act more and more as a world troubleshooter. I told him I intended to take you with me. He agreed.'

My heart leapt. 'That's fantastic!' I said.

'Yes, but you must understand we will not be able to let go like this.'

'Why?' I said, looking at him sadly.

'Because when we do, we become vulnerable, off-guard, and that spells danger. Not only to the Department, but to everyone in it and associated with it.'

'I understand. Are you saying that we'll have to be on parade?'

'I'm saying more than that. I will have to be remote from you, totally controlled at all times – and so will you. That is how it will be if you come with me. Now you have to decide if you still want to come. Don't answer now. I'll ask you again after we're back in London. Think very hard about it. One, can you do it? Two, do you want to?'

He paused. 'For now, let's forget about it. I know somewhere wonderful back in Geneva where we can have dinner.'

And of course he did. Quaint and typically Swiss, it was called L'Auberge de la Mère Royaume and was in a little back street. It was not a well-known restaurant; it was the kind of place you would never find unless you knew about it.

The evening passed in a haze of happiness. True to his word, Peter said no more about what we had discussed, and I didn't ask.

Far too quickly we were on our way back to London in Peter's private jet. He took the controls and, sitting next to him, I even managed to forget that I was nervous of flying. But when we arrived in London, almost before the wheels touched the runway, he changed. Like a polar bear that had been lying on a rock in the sun, he dived back into the depths of his hunting ground. Back into the icy cold.

As soon as the plane landed and we were stationary, he was issuing orders in his usual crisp, no-nonsense way and that included me.

'Helen, follow me.'

'Yes, sir.' It was automatic. He didn't have to tell me we were on parade.

His car was at the bottom of the gangway and Neil appeared as if from nowhere. He briefed Peter on events all the way into London. It struck me how quickly Peter had to don the cloak of confidence, authority and power. There was no hint of any vulnerability now. I wondered what would happen if the polar bear was never able to come up into the sunlight again.

I felt a sudden surge of anger that ordinary people could go safely about their business because this man was prepared to do whatever was necessary to protect them. I knew that he had chosen this but, knowing him now as well as I did, I was really afraid for him.

Most people believed he was untouched by it all, but I knew different. I had seen the smoking, the constant need for a drink. I had never seen him drunk, I believe he only used it as an anaesthetic but still, he drank and smoked too much. It didn't surprise me; in some ways it was reassuring. If he had not done those things, or endured those nightmares that I still witnessed, I would have believed he was inhuman, a machine.

I felt impotent, unable to do anything about it except love him. I just prayed that I would be allowed to do so, and that it would be enough.

When we arrived at Peter's house we went straight into a meeting which lasted well into the afternoon. When everyone had gone, at last we were able to relax again.

That evening we managed to recapture the mood we had generated in Geneva, though I knew it would be fleeting. Peter had booked us a box to see the ballet at Covent Garden, and Margot Fonteyn and Rudolf Nureyev were dancing that night. Tickets were like gold dust and had been sold out in London for months, but somehow Peter had weaved his magic again.

It was the greatest performance I had – and have – ever seen. Rudolf Nureyev is still probably the greatest dancer the world has ever known, and that night he took Fonteyn to heights of perfection far beyond anything she had been before.

It was a gala performance and when Nureyev leapt onto the stage for the first time in 'Le Corsaire', an electric bolt shot through the audience. He was unbelievably sensual and I understood why this dance had almost become his property.

But if I thought his spectacular entrance was the height of the performance, I had not yet seen him dance 'Marguerite and Armand' with Margot Fonteyn. This was specially choreographed for them by Sir Frederick Ashton, and their love for each other shone through the dancing. On the stage that night, they were lovers.

At the end, the audience would not let them go. Nureyev, the perfect showman, came back again and again and presented Fonteyn as the star. The audience threw daffodils, roses, tulips – the stage was awash with flowers. Nureyev gathered them up in armfuls, knelt before Fonteyn and presented her with more and more flowers. The audience were on their feet, loving every minute.

I looked around. People were crying, aware that they had seen something so unique, they would remember it for the rest of their lives.

I turned and looked at Peter and saw tears. He put his arm around me. I was choked with my own tears, but now my tears had changed, now they were for him. At least tonight, I thought, he was in a place and with someone he felt it safe to be himself. My tears were for him, and for us, because I knew that this night was unique, that there would be very few – if any – like it in the future. Tomorrow he would have to close down again totally. We might never know when it would be safe again to express what we really felt.

That night, the beauty and love in the performance on stage matched our feelings for each other.

I know that Peter found it almost impossible to come back from that night. He had a tremendous struggle and, because of that, I didn't see him again for nearly a month. That's how tenuous my life with him was. If he had not succeeded in regaining the control he needed, I would probably never have seen him again.

The curtain finally came down for the last time and even the continuous applause could not bring the two stars out again. People began to leave, and I thought we would too. We got up and left our box but, instead of turning right to the exit, Peter steered me left.

'Where are we going?' my curious self said.

Peter smiled but said nothing. He put his arm around me and ushered me through a door and there we were, behind the stage. People were rushing hither and thither, their arms full of costumes, stage props, messages, everything you can imagine. Peter guided me towards a door clearly marked PRIVATE and knocked smartly. The door was opened by a man who said, 'Good evening, sir. Come this way.'

We walked through it into a corridor, then reached another door across which I saw emblazoned RUDOLF NUREYEV. The man asked us to wait as he tapped on the door and went inside without waiting for a response. He came out almost immediately and held the door open for us to go in.

Nureyev was sitting in front of a mirror. He had changed from his stage costume and was now wearing leggings with a tunic top, and smothering his face with some kind of cream from a large pot in front of him. Grabbing some tissues from a long roll, he began to wipe off his make-up.

He looked at us in the mirror and said in guttural English, 'I won't be a minute, my friend.'

I was astounded. I had no idea he was Peter's friend. So this was how Peter had got the tickets.

Peter said something to Nureyev in what I

presumed was Russian. I looked around the room. On the far side was a rail with all his costumes; opposite that, a large couch. The wall next to where he was sitting was one huge mirror which went from floor to ceiling and had a bar along one side. The dressing table in front of him was covered with various brushes, pots and make-up, and other paraphernalia. Apart from in front of the mirror, every available bit of space seemed to be filled with bouquets of flowers, cards and telegrams.

The room smelt of a mixture of flowers, grease paint and male sweat. It was a heady combination. So this was what it was like to be a star.

Suddenly Nureyev, like a dervish, bounced off his chair and turned towards us.

'Hello. Who's this?' Pointing at me, he said, 'Are you coming to my party?'

'This is Helen and yes we are, Rudi. You were pretty damn good tonight.'

'Yes, I was, wasn't I?'

He loped up to me like a panther and kissed my hand. Then he turned in front of the long mirror and did a couple of *pliés* as if it were the most natural thing in the world.

I felt as if I had landed in the middle of some fairy-tale, like Alice in Wonderland when she went down the hole after the white rabbit. Nureyev sat us down and started talking ten to the dozen in his rather crude English, interspersed with a few words of French. I was enchanted.

Peter replied mixing French with Russian and English. I was even more enchanted.

As I sat and watched them, it occurred to me that I was with probably two of the most sexually attractive men on earth. Yet they were so opposite – or were they? That was a thought. Rudi, with his wide, flaring nostrils and even wider cheekbones, his animal passion. He was virile and oversensitive, a fiery young Russian dancer placed beside this cool epitome of an Englishman.

The Englishman was highly educated, a sophisticated man of the world. The Russian, at that time, was little more than a rough peasant. But they were both tough survivors. Both men had wills of iron and absolute control over themselves. Both adored music, art, culture, and were highly sensitive to the aesthetic world. Both were proud, arrogant men, isolated and lonely.

I asked Peter afterwards how he knew Nureyev.

'Well,' he told me, 'someone had to check up on him when he came West. Someone who could understand him. His English was appalling, even his Russian was a dialect that was almost incomprehensible. Then there was the fact that, sexually, we knew he swung both ways.

'Oh,' I said naively, 'but he seems to be in love with Margot Fonteyn.'

'Helen, things are not always as they seem. They are together at the moment but nothing will ever come of it.'

'Why not?'

'Rudi is too artistic, too temperamental. She is much older than him. She is also married to a very powerful man. The situation is fraught with danger. Her husband had numerous affairs, and is now in a wheelchair after having been shot by a jealous spouse. Rudi is having an artistic love affair – not a real one. Creative people are like that. It's not real, Helen, it's an illusion ...' He paused.

'But a very beautiful one,' I said.

I never saw Nureyev again, but I followed his life and career closely and was sad to see him ravaged by AIDS many years later.

It was never confirmed to me, but I believe when

he came over he passed useful information to the West and continued to do so. In return he was protected from the Russians.

# Chapter 21
# The Reply

By the next day I was back home in Cheshire. As soon as I could I went to see Jessie and told her everything that had happened, omitting, of course, any reference to who Peter really was.

'Darling, it appears you managed beautifully,' she said. 'So what are you asking me?'

'Yes, Jessie, but how shall I answer his question?'

'Well, of course you must go, you silly girl! You don't need to ask me that.' She planted a kiss right on the end of my nose. 'You will go because you will be with him. You will meet wonderful and interesting people, you'll have a fantastic experience, and you will love him so he's not alone. I'm proud of you, I love you and just remember, I'm always here for you whenever you want me.'

I put my arms around her and gave her a big hug. We spent the day together laughing and joking as we always did. Jessie was now in her seventies but she still had more energy than anyone I have ever met. She could walk me off my feet with no trouble at all.

Later, we were in the car coming back from a long walk when Jessie asked me, 'Have you got a photo of him?'

I hesitated. 'Yes.'

'Can I see it?'

I trusted her and decided to take the risk, so once we were back at the house, I showed her the only recent photo I had of Peter. He had agreed to give me one when I promised not to keep it in my handbag or on show at home, so I had hidden it carefully in my bookcase upstairs. It showed him sitting on his Chesterfield in the drawing room of his London home, a brandy goblet in one hand, a cigarette in its black ebony holder in the other. It was a pose I had seen him in many times.

When I handed the photo to Jessie, she exclaimed, 'Oh my dear! He's quite, quite glorious!' She grinned. 'Men are so lucky, the years usually add to the good-looking ones, while we women...' She shrugged.

I looked closely at her. Had she recognised him? If so, she gave nothing away.

'Jessie, it isn't just his looks that makes him so attractive. It's the way he dresses, the way he carries himself, the way he speaks, the way he is, everything about him.'

'Yes, my dear, but you have that too. You must make a sensational couple.'

'Oh rubbish!' I said. Although I didn't believe her, it was lovely to hear it all the same.

'So when are you going to answer his question?'

'I don't know. He said he would contact me. I'll have to wait.'

Little did I know that I would have to wait for nearly a month. Our time together in Geneva, and then at the ballet, had opened a door he was having tremendous difficulty in closing, and he wasn't prepared to see me again until he had done so. In the meantime I was left in Cheshire, wondering where he was.

Just as I was beginning to think he was never going to contact me again, Neil phoned.

'Can you meet Peter at Manchester Airport tomorrow at 2 pm? He'll be in his own plane.'

'Of course,' I said.

'I'll see you at 2 pm then.' The phone clicked off.

I was there at the appointed time. It was a boiling hot sunny day without a breath of air and I was wearing a wide-brimmed sun hat; being so fair, I'd always had to be very careful with the sun. I watched the planes landing through a cloudless sky and at exactly five minutes to two o'clock, I recognised Peter's as it approached the runway. When you love someone so much, you recognise things earlier: the small things, a certain style.

I could imagine him behind the controls and I suddenly felt nervous – more nervous that usual because I wasn't sure after Geneva exactly how we were going to operate. I quickly decided that 'on parade' was the safest place to be until I was told otherwise. I locked into control as I had been trained, although my feelings were all over the place. I wanted to cry, but I didn't know why.

Luckily at that moment Neil appeared.

'Come on, Helen, let's go.' He marched out towards the aircraft and I followed, hanging on to my hat, which now threatened to blow away with the wind that is always present on runways. As we reached the plane they released the steps and I followed Neil inside. But when he disappeared into the cockpit, I didn't follow; I sat down and waited.

In just a few moments Peter appeared. As I saw him I thought: Why do I always feel as if I'm in the presence of a king?

I stood up. 'Good afternoon, sir.'

'Good afternoon, Helen.' He came forward and gave me a kiss. 'Relax,' he said, 'we're off parade.'

When he said that I was relieved that I had made the right decision. It was imperative to let him know that I understood what he had said to me at the end in Geneva.

'I only have a couple of hours, Helen, and then I have to be back in London. But next week I'm going to Southern Rhodesia. Are you coming?' I knew that was his way of asking me for the answer to his question.

'Yes,' I said, 'I'm coming and I know the score.'

He grinned. 'Great,' he said.

We sat in the sitting area of the plane for the next two hours and just talked and talked.

Like our emotional relationship, the way we related sexually had now also changed. Although I hadn't seen Peter for a month, that afternoon he didn't attempt to make love to me. That didn't surprise me. Over the years, when he wanted to be, Peter was a highly sensitive and caring lover. Although he could also be brutal and uncaring, that first time in Marbella had told me forever just how wonderful sex with him could be. Over the years I hung onto the memory of it.

But after Geneva, I only ever experienced the lover I had met in Marbella. That afternoon, under those circumstances, he did not want a hurried coupling. I think he was also confirming to himself the control that he had to assert with a vengeance after Geneva.

At exactly four o'clock Peter left for London and I drove home feeling content. We had moved to a deeper understanding and I was looking forward to and accepting things as they were. I had stopped burying my head in the sand and I felt Peter had stopped fighting against our love.

The next period was to be the happiest time I had experienced in my life so far. I am glad I did not know then how short-lived my happiness would be.

# Chapter 22
# The Ambassador

I had known Peter now for nearly ten years and I was no longer the immature young girl he had met in Spain. Because of him I had become much more sophisticated and worldly. I had learned a tremendous amount from Peter, but I had also educated myself, so I felt confident that I could contribute to his work.

Jessie was right again and over the next months I met some wonderful people – and some terrible ones, even evil. But they were all fascinating, and of course it was an exciting experience for a young woman brought up in the protected environment of an English country home.

The best thing about it was what gradually happened to the relationship between Peter and myself. Yes, we did have to remain in control every time we were on a mission. But a real friendship developed which had not existed before. It was as if having to batten down our emotional and sexual feelings enabled something even deeper to blossom.

Before, we had been lovers with a Svengali/Trilby relationship. Before, I was in awe of him, obsessed with him. I was, as he had said, in the palm of his hand. Now we became more equal. We became true friends. Whereas I had once had him on a pedestal, now, although he never tumbled from that pedestal, I felt as if I had climbed up there alongside him. People treated us both with such respect – not necessarily when we first met them, but always fairly quickly afterwards.

Peter and I grew closer and closer. He had not had a friend since his childhood and he had never had one before of the opposite sex. He loved it and I sensed his delight. We found we were a team who had to rely on each other. Sometimes he would pull us out of a tight spot and at other times it would be me. We had known before that we complemented each other: now we realised there was a synergy between us.

As a woman, I recognised that our initial sexual attraction had overwhelmed us. The love had been there but it was always in danger of being suffocated by a tumultuous passion. Now it was able to breathe and, with more space, it was flourishing. We brought out the best in each other – the highest definition of love. The heart of that love was mutual respect and trust.

I was in my element when I was with him. I was basically a realist with an idealist soul and the whole scenario appeared to have been made for me. Someone once said that a person with great power needs someone next to them with total objectivity. Peter had immense power and I was able at that time to supply the objectivity. As a woman I loved it: loved being beside a powerful man. But now it wasn't in a childlike or subservient way. It felt right. I knew that I added to him; I could ride on his brilliance whilst at the same time enabling him to jump even further. With him, I could literally feel myself growing.

In Southern Rhodesia we met Ian Smith. He was the man who years before had declared UDI, a unilateral declaration of independence against the British Government and then made himself Prime Minister. This was essentially a white dictatorship and an act of treason on his part. Smith had been a wartime fighter pilot and hero, and there was a lot of sympathy for him in Britain, but as a result of the declaration, sanctions were declared against Rhodesia. Smith managed to ride the sanctions but not the internal terrorism that accompanied it.

Now, in the 1970s, it was a question of trying to bring him into line. Peter had a natural rapport with him due to them both having been fighter pilots, but I found him acerbic and grouchy, and did not warm to him. However, when we left Peter had got his agreement in all the areas he wanted. He had reassured Smith that he would not lose face and the result of this and other meetings was that Smith caused very little further trouble when Christopher Soames (the man I had seen as a child dining with Winston Churchill at the Savoy) went in on behalf of the British Government some years later and enabled real independence which enfranchised all races.

With government knowledge, and sometimes unspoken consent, Peter was able to act as an unofficial ambassador. He often had to tread a delicate path, talking behind the scenes with powerbrokers whom the country or the West could not be seen to be dealing with openly.

We went to many countries and met a host of African leaders, some who were benevolent dictators and others, like Idi Amin of Uganda, who were brutal tyrants. Some we met in London or Geneva, others at airport hotels or even inside their private planes on some obscure runway.

Some were egomaniacs, others genuine leaders who only wanted to better their fledgling nations. Peter was always patient, always courteous, sometimes for hours on end, and he would win their trust. Then they would listen to him and he would guide them.

There were times when he had a verbal message for them. This could be from the West in general or from Britain in particular. It was always unofficial but delivered in such a way that the recipient had no doubt as to its meaning, or that it would be implemented if necessary. Certainly I know Peter stopped or helped to stop some of the most horrendous happenings in the world at that time.

When I met world leaders I noticed that the successful ones all shared things in common with the Department. Over the years Peter's influence had borne fruit.

Peter also met the man who was to become the last white President of South Africa. He talked to Peter when he was first working out how, if he ever had the opportunity, he would deal with leading his country out of apartheid. He told Peter that he would have three main problems: timing, timing and timing. He and Peter quickly found themselves on the same wavelength.

Years later the world watched fascinated as FW de Klerk became Prime Minister and began to dismantle apartheid. I noted just how brilliant his timing was. He never got it wrong, from the release of Nelson Mandela to the gradual erosion of the apartheid system and all it stood for. His ultimate act as leader of the country he loved was to have the humility and control to stand down and be Deputy Leader. I believe most other men would have disappeared from the scene as fast as they could.

Peter's connections were not influenced by changes of government or top personnel. Churchill had set him up in the early 1950s with introductions, and the Prime Minister's own standing in the world at that time was so great that all other leaders were prepared to give an audience to someone sent in his name.

Peter then quickly built up his own reputation and by the time I was with him he was totally respected in his own right.

It was heady stuff for me to be involved with such people. They asked for advice and listened to what he had to say. Peter always, without fail, gave credit to

Great Britain. He wanted to build on our standing on the world stage as an experienced and mature nation. He was not afraid to be critical when necessary. There were occasions when he gave some of the newly-formed African states a very straight talking to.

I remember one night when he came back to our hotel, he grinned at me and said, 'I think it might be wise, Helen, if we go to the airport right now and get the hell out of here!' And we did.

When we got back to London, it didn't matter what time of the day of night it was; if it was necessary, he would pick up the phone and make sure the Prime Minister was fully briefed. There was never any question of Peter feeling he had to justify or explain anything that had happened, but sometimes it was necessary to give information.

What I picked up from these meetings was the vulnerability, loneliness, sometimes even fear, of these powerful men. To begin with it shook me. After all, didn't they have the world in their hands? I had always believed they must be inviolate.

This was not true. They were ordinary men who had been voted into, pushed into, or had seized extraordinary power. Some of them were good men, some were great men, but they were still just men with strengths, weaknesses and feelings like everyone else.

One of Peter's gifts was that he could very quickly make them believe he had some of the answers to their doubts and fears. His greatest gift was that he *did* have answers.

I was right there beside him as he influenced world events. Today I sometimes find it hard to believe that an ordinary English girl could have found herself in such a position.

Today I hear about some of these incidents and events and I know what is being reported is a distortion of certain facts, or the whole truth, or both. Sometimes it is downright lies.

There appears to be an element of the British psyche that has a need to denigrate our own heroes, our own history, or deny that anything brilliant ever originated from this country. It has spawned a culture that enjoys running down everything and anything we do. Over the years the Intelligence Services have suffered from this and have continually been reported as being amateur and at times even stupid.

Surprisingly, Peter actively encouraged this view. It was useful, he explained, because it made everyone underestimate how competent our Intelligence Services really were, which gave them a certain edge. Let the world see a poorly-run, infiltrated service; behind the scenes we had the finest in the world.

I have watched programmes and read articles that purport to tell the truth about certain events involving British Intelligence. The media seem determined to give their own interpretation in order to cause as much controversy as possible. They are motivated by the drive for higher ratings and more profit, under the guise of 'getting to the truth'.

Peter always felt that it was fair to play them at their own game. What mattered to him was not how highly Britain's intelligence services were regarded by the outside world, but the advantage this country gained by continually confirming the world's perception of its incompetent intelligence network. The feeding of misinformation was therefore rife and apparently still is.

This was one of the things I found very difficult. I did care what the outside world thought, and I still do. It is another weakness I never did learn to control.

In Britain, Peter's influence cut across any party allegiances. It didn't matter which party was in power, certainly not to him or to the Department. Prime Ministers came and went and on the whole they were grateful and relieved to find the Department, although from time to time they had to state publicly in the House of Commons that 'the Department that didn't exist' really didn't.

When we travelled, Peter allowed others back in London to hold the fort and run the Department in his absence. Sometimes he still made the decisions, but I noticed that he often encouraged his team to go it alone.

When we returned to London, he would review what had been done. If it had gone wrong he would ask the questions that would enable his team to work out for themselves why. He rarely needed to show his anger. If people let him down they knew it – just a word or a glance was enough. When they got it right it was the same. His standards were exacting, but they brought out the very best in the people around him. The respect for him was absolute.

Over the years Peter's involvement with America continued and this 'special relationship' was extremely healthy. He was in touch almost on a daily basis with everyone who held any real power in the United States, from the President downwards. The relationship between the two countries was far, far closer than I had ever imagined; it was so positive and I still believe today that America, not Europe, is our natural ally. Most of the European countries have little in common with us. They do not understand us, an island people, and not a few dislike us intensely. America and Britain are more like family – they quarrel but when threatened from the outside, they are drawn together like opposite poles of a magnet.

I suspect that the Americans also had a similar Department within their intelligence services. Like our own it could have been developed after the war from the remains of the Office of Strategic Services, or OSS as it was more commonly known. This was the equivalent of the British SOE.

With all I saw and participated in, it would have been easy to get carried away, but Peter had the knack of keeping one's feet firmly on the ground. He did not judge people by their position, or the amount of money or power they had; that counted for nothing. When you were with him, you operated on his value system, and he judged people by their actions. Power could be fickle, titles a mask and money a false friend. A man could lie, but action was action. I saw 'big' people who were nothing and 'little' people who were heroes.

When you were with Peter, it was almost impossible to be impressed by the wrong things. He decimated that kind of nonsense.

During this time I began to get deeper into Peter's psyche. We had long philosophical conversations which opened up totally new areas of thought to me. I would question Peter endlessly. I loved the agility of his mind and the depth and experience of his views. I loved the way he would toss ideas around and toy with alternatives, finally resting on one but never negating further discussion.

'Are you a spy?' I asked one day.

'What is a spy?' he said, mildly amused.

'Someone who works undercover to protect their country,' I said earnestly.

'How do you define "their country", Helen? Is it where they live, where they have citizenship, or even what they believe is their country? How do you judge if someone is a legitimate spy or a traitor?'

'Well,' I said confidently, 'a traitor is someone who betrays his country.'

'So the fifty-six men who signed the Declaration of Independence for America were all traitors?

Cromwell was a traitor? Ian Smith in Southern Rhodesia was a traitor?'

That made me think!

'You need to be very careful how you define treachery and treason.'

'How would you define them?' I said, curious.

'Firstly I would have to explain my definition of country – then my definition of loyalty to my country – only then could I explain my definition of a traitor.'

'So, what *is* your definition of your country?'

'For me, Helen, that is simple. I am lucky. I was born an Englishman, I live in England, I believe myself to be English. For other people it is not so simple. You need to understand that.'

When I asked him to explain, he asked me to consider the Indian living in England. If he was born here he might feel very English, but where was his loyalty? If he had emigrated here but his children were born here, it might be even more complex.

Then there were religious beliefs. Ask an English Jew living in England whether he is a Jew first or an Englishman first.

I agreed it was much more complicated than I had thought. So how, I wondered, would he define loyalty to his country?

'This is one of my strongest reasons for retaining the monarchy,' Peter said. 'If it did not exist, one's loyalty could be torn between the state, the government of the day, the law of the land, one's religion, one's nationality. The monarchy removes that conflict. One swears allegiance to the monarch, not the state. I am loyal to the monarchy as embodied in our unwritten constitution. To understand completely you need to distinguish between the function of monarchy and the Royal Family itself. The former gives us objectivity, a stability and continuity that reaches back over a thousand years; the latter gives us subjectivity, good and bad monarchs who attempt in their own way to fulfil that function.'

He explained that the division of political and constitutional power gave the right balance. Monarchy, he said, was the sheet anchor of the nation, and the monarch as head of state had constitutional power and responsibility. The Prime Minister had the political power and each was inter-dependent

'Why is the constitution unwritten?' I asked him.

'We prefer it that way in Britain. It enables flexibility and we can thereby adapt the constitution to the needs of an evolving nation. It stops the lawyers getting hold of it and picking it to bits. I believe it would be a backward step if we ever attempted to have a written constitution.'

When I asked him to define treachery, he became even more thoughtful.

'That's very complicated. First I would have to answer the other questions. To start, do you consider members of the IRA to be traitors?'

'I don't know,' I said, after weighing this question against the others.

'They believe themselves to be Irish. Southern Ireland is not a part of Great Britain, therefore they are not answerable to the British state. If they are from Southern Ireland, strictly speaking they are enemies of Great Britain, not traitors. If they are from Northern Ireland, which is part of Great Britain, it becomes more complicated.'

We discussed what he defined as clear-cut cases of treachery – people like Burgess or Maclean. They were British, they had worked for a government department and had sworn allegiance to the Queen. But when he asked me if I thought Claus von Stauffenburg and his co-conspirators, the Germans who had tried to assassinate Hitler, were traitors, I missed the complexity.

216

'Well,' I said, 'they were German. They lived in Germany. They were in the Army so they must have sworn loyalty to the state. So yes, it looks as if they were traitors.' I smiled, quite pleased with myself.

Peter smiled back and shook his head. 'Not in my eyes they weren't. They were Germans living in Germany. They were in the Army and they had actually sworn allegiance to Hitler personally. However, Hitler had grabbed absolute power by illegally changing the constitution. He was therefore not representing the people. Stauffenberg and his co-conspirators were loyal to Germany, so in my eyes they were not traitors. They were patriots and heroes.'

I recalled the writer E M Forster saying: 'If I had to choose between betraying my country and betraying my friend, I hope I would have the guts to betray my country.' What did Peter think of that?

'I think it's appalling,' he said, 'but if you can't define your country and it's therefore of little importance to you, I suppose it's understandable that your loyalty might be with your friend. For some people it could be an agonising choice. For me it would be very clear. I would not hesitate to kill my friend.'

I was fascinated. I had imagined that someone in Peter's position would have been much more black and white about such matters, even as they applied to other people, and it was a revelation to find that he wasn't. It was also reassuring that he was so definite about where he himself stood.

I was still determined to return to my initial question. 'So, are you a spy?' I said boldly.

His smile this time was indulgent. The dictionary, he said, defined a spy as a person employed by the state or an institution to obtain secret information from rival countries, organisations or companies, and by that definition he was definitely not a spy. He was

217

not employed by anyone and he did not go around obtaining secret information.

'So how would you define who you are and what you do?' I insisted.

I could see he was mildly amused by my determination. Eventually he said, 'I am a patriot. I work in the background doing whatever is necessary to protect and promote this country throughout the world.'

'Is that it?'

'Yes, Helen – it really is as simple as that. Exquisitely simple and absolute. There is no compromise, no half measures. I am totally committed to that objective.'

Now he *was* black and white. I looked at him. His face had that icy expression I recognised: eyes slightly narrowed, mouth set.

'What made you a patriot?' I asked.

'My love of England, of Great Britain – but England is the heart of Great Britain.'

When I asked him what he loved so much about this country, he told me that to answer that, one needed to have an understanding of history. History gives a country a long-term perspective of itself, its character and make-up. It teaches understanding of the evolution of a nation and tells its people where they have come from and where they now belong. It helps them to see what sort of people they are, gives a rationale for the love of their country, a feeling for it.

'That's one thing that made me a patriot,' he said. 'I love the Englishness of the English. They do not shout about their nationality. It is there, unstated. They have no need to prove it; they take it for granted. This is both a strength and a weakness. We leave things until we are under dire threat and then realise almost too late that our liberty, our very Englishness, are in peril. So often it is only at the very last moment that we stand up and are counted.'

'So what's your definition of "Englishness"?' I persisted.

'If anyone should know the answer to that, you should!' he smiled tolerantly.

Then he became pensive. 'Fundamentally we are an island people, a nation of individuals. We detest the collective herd and yet we are disciplined and ordered. This discipline needs to come from the people rather than the state. In most other countries it is the other way round. The state demands the discipline and order and the people comply.

'We are an old, mature civilisation. Because we had an empire, we learned the virtues of tolerance, patience and empathy. Eventually we learned that the best way to rule was to enable others to rule themselves, to grow up and become independent sovereign nations. Along the way we sometimes got it wrong.

'We still act today as if we have a civilising mission in the world. In the days of the empire it was mostly benevolent; now it is reflected in the way we look after the poor in Third World countries.'

He saw he had my full attention and continued. 'Englishness is based on respect for the individual, freedom of speech and freedom to allow people to do things in their own way. English values are based on duty, honour and integrity. Never doubt these values are still there, underpinning our beliefs.'

Peter saw the English as a proud and courageous people who displayed certain paradoxes. They had an arrogance based on feelings of superiority, yet went through long periods of self-doubt; a coolness that signalled to people to keep their distance; a calm and phlegmatic nature that was reassuring to themselves but could be quite bewildering to others. Because of their tolerance, he believed, they allowed elements of society to sink into extremism, provided they remained within the law. The silent majority was often totally opposed to this element but it kept quiet because it believed people can agree to disagree. Ours was a mature civilisation that could accommodate difference.

Peter was convinced that, in the end, it was this very tolerance that thwarted the potential for aggression. Extremists realised they were ranting and raging in a vacuum, tilting at windmills. They were their own audience; nobody else was taking much notice of them. This allowed them to burn out their angst.

From time to time, the extremism had to be released. It expressed the anger, the black emotionalism, the radicalism of some of the nation. Once it had made itself heard, we could come back to the centre ground, to the silent majority.

Peter believed the extremists often provided the avant garde ideas and frenetic energy that balanced the general conservatism of the English. These two opposites allowed our society to evolve safely, without going off the rails.

The Department had to be aware of extremism and help keep it within safe bounds. Peter had to determine when the Department should act to protect Britain, as it was vital not to be out of step with the nation.

I thought again of his emphasis on control and timing. Planning and preparing was one thing but knowing the time to act was quite another.

Peter also maintained that our English humour was a great asset. It quickly deflated tension, went right to the heart of problems and enabled us to see and laugh at the funny side of ourselves.

But there was one thing I still had not asked him. 'Why do you do it?'

He looked puzzled. 'What do you mean?'

'What made you make this your whole life?'

'No-one has ever asked me that before.' He paused.

When he finally did speak, it was another revelation. 'It gave me something to live for.'

'That you thought wouldn't hurt you?'

His fists clenched and he stiffened. I thought I had gone too far.

'You're ... very perceptive,' he said slowly. There was a silence, then he continued: 'It gave meaning to my life. It gave me an outlet for all sorts of things that I was good at. It quenched a thirst. Then it claimed me, and now it has my soul.'

'Like a religious belief?'

'Stronger than that. Now it's part of me. Now it *is* me.'

## Chapter 23
## Farewell

What happened next I had blanked out until now. But when I started writing this book, I always knew I would have to come to it.

As I write this chapter I am allowing myself to remember. Perhaps when I have finished, the jigsaw will be complete, because up to now there are many things I have avoided and still don't understand.

The children were home from boarding school on their summer holidays. I never travelled with Peter when they were at home. It annoyed him sometimes, I knew, but he had come to accept it. Now they were boarding, holidays were sacrosanct.

So I hadn't seen him for nearly two months. We had talked endlessly on the phone and I had arranged to meet him in London two days after the children's return to school. On the phone he had sounded cheerful and his normal self, so I suspected nothing when Neil met me as arranged at Euston Station. It was only when we were safely ensconced in a taxi, edging its way through the London traffic, that I sensed something was wrong.

'What's happened, Neil?'

'It's Peter, Helen – he's ill, very ill.'

I felt myself go cold. 'What do you mean – what's the matter?'

'I'm sorry, Helen, I don't know any other way to tell you this, he's got cancer.' He said no more.

'Neil – Neil, talk to me. Where? How? How long has he known? Is it curable?'

He ignored all but the last question and shook his head. 'No – no, Helen, it's not. It's in the liver and it's spread all over his body. It's only a question of months.'

I shook my head at him. 'But why didn't I know, why didn't anyone tell me?'

'He ordered us not to. He knew your children were on holiday and he wanted you to enjoy them. He knew you would come today as soon as they were back at school. He only discharged himself from hospital yesterday.'

'Oh Neil!' I heard myself cry in anguish.

'I'm so sorry, Helen.'

I was stunned, unable to speak. Anyway, I didn't know what to say. Neil sat hunched in the corner of the taxi. He looked defeated.

The taxi arrived and, leaving Neil to settle the fare with the driver, I jumped out and ran up the steps. The door swung open. I ran straight past the man who had opened it and up the stairs. At the top I turned left and, without knocking, flung open the doors to the drawing room.

It was empty. The red velvet Chesterfield looked lost without him sitting there with his brandy goblet in one hand and his ebony cigarette holder in the other.

I ran up the next flight of steps to his bedroom. That was empty too – so were the dressing room and bathroom.

Coming down the stairs again I met Neil. 'Where is he? Oh, Neil where is he?'

'Helen. Steady, calm yourself. He's in the study.'

Ignoring him, I tore past and stopped in front of the study doors. I knocked but didn't wait for an answer. I opened the double doors and walked in. As soon as I saw him, I calmed.

Peter was on the far side of the room, taking a book down from the bookcase. He put it on the table and turned to smile at me. For a moment I thought it was all a mistake. I walked over to him but as I got closer and he turned further into the light from the window, I saw his features full on.

I was appalled. He looked desperately ill and had lost a frightening amount of weight. His eyes seemed to have sunk into their sockets, his face was drawn and the dimples were very pronounced as he smiled at me. What was most disturbing was his skin. It was waxen, with a deep yellow hue.

I tried to conceal my shock and failed miserably.

'Helen, my dear. You look as if you've seen a ghost.' When I did not reply he continued: 'I'm so sorry. Come on, let's go into the drawing room and sit down. I'll ask Paul to bring you some coffee.'

He took my arm and led me across the hall and through some doors into the room opposite. We both sat down and there was silence.

Then, without warning, I began to cry. I tried desperately to stop, but the more I tried, the worse I became, until I gave up. I put my head in my hands and sobbed uncontrollably. Gradually the sobs diminished and I felt something pushed into my hands. It was a silk handkerchief.

'Last time you did this, you silly girl, was in Marbella, and you stole my handkerchief. Make sure you give it back to me this time!'

I looked up. Peter was leaning towards me, one eyebrow raised and that slightly amused look on his face.

'All these years I've been trying to make you cry again in front of me and I have failed. Now you cry when I don't want you to. At least last time you had a good reason to cry; this time you have none, so please stop.'

He was grinning and with a great deal of effort I managed to smile.

'Right – perhaps you need the same cure as last

time. First a large brandy and then I shall make love to you.'

My mouth dropped open. Paul quietly entered the room.

'Paul, please bring a large brandy for Helen. Then make sure nothing disturbs us until the doctor comes at two o'clock.'

'Yes, sir.'

He returned shortly and discreetly set down a tray with the brandy on it. Peter handed it to me.

'Drink, Helen, or I shall put you on parade.'

I did as I was told.

True to his word, a little later Peter took me upstairs and we made love. As soon as he touched me I was as lost as ever, lost in the place where I had found myself. Lost where I wanted to be lost. Lost so that he could find me and transport me into his world, a world I had never known in any sense until I met him but one I now wanted to stay in forever.

Afterwards, he gently told me how much he loved me and then, as we so often did, we fell asleep. I woke to a discreet knock at the door and Paul's voice calling out, 'Sir, the doctor's here.'

Peter turned to me. 'Helen wait downstairs, I'll see you later.'

His voice was gentle. Quickly I left the bed and went into his dressing room, taking my clothes with me. After I had washed and dressed I went downstairs into the drawing-room and waited. My mind felt as if it were frozen. I was not conscious of time, but sometime later the doctor came down to speak to me. He explained that there was very little they could do but as the disease progressed they were giving Peter drugs to relieve the pain.

'He's weakening all the time and he's in some pain. I don't think it will be more that a couple of months, maybe three.'

'Can he stay here?' I asked.

'Yes – we have everything we need. I've ordered nursing care around the clock for when it becomes necessary.'

After a few more questions he got up. I shook his hand and thanked him, then he left.

I rushed back upstairs, not waiting for permission. Entering the bedroom I saw that Peter was asleep. I walked over to the bed and looked carefully at him, trying to take in the fact that he was dying, but my mind kept blanking out. It was like a picture that won't stay on the television screen.

When I saw again how ill he looked I remembered the lovemaking and it occurred to me how determined he must have been to do that. It was such a beautiful thing to do, yet it must have taken a lot out of him.

I kissed him gently on the forehead and sat down on the bed beside him. How long I sat there I don't know. It was unimportant. There was nowhere else I wanted to be. There were no difficult decisions to be made; Peter appeared to making those for me. I was so grateful.

It was late summer and the evenings were long but as the sun went down I felt the room grow cooler. I got up quietly and went to close the window. When I turned back he was awake.

'My darling.' The unfamiliar endearment registered. 'Come here and sit on the bed. I must talk to you.' He patted the cover and I sat down.

'There are some instructions I must give you. It's important that you do exactly as I say.'

I nodded.

'Tonight, go to the Savoy Hotel. There is a suite booked for you on the fourth floor. Wait there until Neil comes. It will be sometime tomorrow.'

'Can't I stay with you – please?' I pleaded.

'No. We will say goodbye shortly.'

The word 'goodbye' hit me like a blow and I visibly flinched. I didn't quite understand but of course he knew that. He took my hands.

'When Neil comes you will understand. Remember everything he says to you comes directly from me. You once said that you trusted me with your life and I told you you were stupid. Do you remember?' I nodded. 'You worried me then because you were right, but I could not afford for you to know that. I had to make you believe that I would always put the Department first, that it was not even an issue. Then I had to make quite sure that I never put us in a position where I had to choose between you and the Department. It was a choice I wasn't prepared to make.

'It didn't matter what you said or what you did,' I said. 'I still trusted you with my life anyway. I have always trusted you from the first night in Spain. Whatever happened afterwards, I knew that was the real you.'

He smiled. 'Did you now! That was very clever of you because of course you were right. I gave myself away that night.' He paused and then continued. 'So when Neil comes, understand he is acting on my orders. You're still young, Helen. You must regain your life. I will clear the way and give you everything you need to do so, but you must pick up what I give you. You won't like what happens but you will have to trust me. Don't try to go against what Neil tells you. Remember it is all being done on my orders. Eventually you will understand.'

He paused again. 'Soon I want you to go.'

'All right, but I'll come back tomorrow.'

'Do as Neil says – promise me.'

'Yes – yes, I promise.'

'Before you go I want to read something to you. When I've finished you must go. Will you do as I say?'

I nodded, remembering. *I will do whatever you say.* Suddenly it dawned on me that this was a final goodbye. As if this goodbye could be anything else.

Peter smiled. How can you smile, I thought? How do you leave a man you love so much? How do you smile and leave? How do you leave at all?

He was talking again. 'Good. Fetch me the book I put on the table in the study when you arrived.'

Reluctantly I got up and went to the door but before leaving I turned back to him.

'You know,' I said, 'one day *I'm* going to write a book – about you.'

His expression was tender. 'Well, you might just do that, but you'll have to wait a long time – at least thirty years.'

When I still lingered he urged me, 'Go.'

Entering the study I saw the book where he had left it on the table. I picked it up: it was *A Tale of Two Cities* by Charles Dickens. Part of me wanted to rush back upstairs as fast as I could so that I could be with him. The other wanted to stay here so that I could prolong for as long as possible the moment when I would have to leave.

I knew he was helping me, and that without that help I would never be able to leave. He had always understood me better that I understood myself. Even now, because I needed him to be, he was in charge.

I found myself outside the bedroom door. Gripping the book tightly I entered, forcing a smile as I went to hand it to him.

'Draw up a chair and sit there,' he said. I realised afterwards that, even then, he was beginning to distance himself from me.

I did as he said and he opened the book and began turning the pages. Finally he stopped at a page and his features seemed to relax. Slowly he began to read but I saw it was not from the book. It was from a piece of paper bearing his own handwriting that had been tucked away inside.

'In the hour of my death I shall hold sacred the one good remembrance and shall thank and bless you for it: that my name and memory will always be gently carried in your heart. You have been part of my existence, part of myself. You have been in my every thought since I first saw you; the young woman whose heart I wounded even then.

'You have been the embodiment of every graceful fancy that my mind has ever become acquainted with. You cannot choose now but remain part of my character, part of the good in me, part of the bad.

'Thank you for showing me how glorious a thing it is to love and be loved.' The room fell silent, then he spoke again. 'Go now, my love.'

I got up. I kissed first his lips out of love, and then the back of his hand out of respect. 'I will always love you,' I said. 'I will carry you gently in my heart forever.'

I walked to the door and spoke again. 'Thank you for allowing me into your heart. Thank you for giving me my life. Goodbye.'

'Goodbye,' he said.

I closed the door quietly and walked away. I didn't look back. I knew the last thing I could do for him was to leave him with dignity, but it was the hardest thing I have ever done.

I never saw Peter again.

I wasn't at all brave. I could not face the pain; it was too vast. I ran from it, blocked it out, refused to countenance it. I don't remember arriving at The Savoy, or anything else about that night after I left Peter. I was on automatic pilot, programmed, thank God, to obey him.

The next day was also a blur until sometime late that afternoon. I remember sitting looking out over the Thames at all the people rushing to the tube station in the embankment gardens below, anxious to get home. I remember wanting desperately to go back to Peter and having to force myself to stay where I was, knowing that he trusted me to do as he asked.

It was just beginning to go dark when the phone rang. 'It's Neil. I'm in the foyer. Can I come up?'

'Yes.' I heard myself almost choke on the words.

I knew he was dead. I don't know how but I knew with absolute certainty. I also knew that Neil would give me the answers.

I opened the door and saw him striding along the corridor towards me. I couldn't help it; I ran to meet him. Before he had a chance to say what I knew he must, I threw myself into his arms. He caught me and held me tight.

I didn't cry. I couldn't. It was more like the keening of an animal in pain. Firmly Neil guided me back into my room and, after lowering me into a chair, he fetched a glass of water.

'Take these,' he said, handing me two tablets and the water. I swallowed them.

'When?' I asked.

'About two hours ago.'

I had stopped the keening but now I was rocking backwards and forwards in the chair. I struggled to stop.

'How?'

'Like his life, Helen, he had control over his death. He was just waiting to see you first and then he took care of it. It was completely in keeping with the man. He died as he lived, with great dignity.'

I tried to take that in.

'When did you last eat?'

'I don't know.'

'Today?' I shook my head. 'Yesterday?'

'No.'

'Hmm' He rang a bell on the wall for room service.
'I can't eat.'

'Peter said you would follow his instructions.' He smiled gently. 'You took the tablets. Now you'll eat – then we'll talk.'

And at the sound of his name I started to cry – quite softly, but I could feel it was coming from somewhere very deep inside me. Neil came up to me immediately and took me back in his arms. There was a knock at the door.

'Room service, sir.'

Neil ordered two bowls of chicken soup, a plate of mixed sandwiches and a large pot of tea. When the waiter had gone, Neil held me until the tears subsided. He didn't say anything and it was better that way. Later, after I had attempted to eat a little and the pills had taken effect, he talked to me.

'Before he died Peter gave me instructions concerning you. You won't like them.'

'I know,' I said softly, 'but I'll do whatever he says.'

He nodded, not realising the significance of the words.

'Even now, as we talk, the Department no longer exists for you and it never has. It was never there. Anything you may remember or talk about will be pure fantasy on your part: all phone numbers, contacts etc are dead. You are to have no contact with anyone. All connections are cut forthwith and forever.'

'I understand.'

'That includes me as well. I will take you home tomorrow and then that's it. We have never known each other.'

I was silent. That was a blow. Somehow I had thought Neil would always be there for me.

'I understand.'

'Do you?'

It was a long time before I answered. Then I said

very slowly, 'No … but I don't have to. If it's what Peter instructed then that's what must happen. I won't question it.'

'Helen, everything he instructed was out of love for you. On the one hand he was determined to protect you, but on the other he wanted to give you back your life. He always felt he stole it from you when you broke his cover.'

I thought about that, it registered.

Neil continued. 'The reality was that he had to, otherwise they would certainly have insisted that you were eliminated. Now you can go back into the real world. As long as we close all the doors, in five years' time you will be free of any connection.'

I heard what he said but I found it hard to accept. I had been very happy with the life that had replaced my so-called 'stolen' life and I wondered if I could ever be happy again.

'The doctor is coming in a minute to give you something to make you sleep. I shall stay here tonight. Can I suggest that you go and get ready for bed. I'll send him into you when he comes. Tomorrow I'll drive you home and we can talk some more then.'

Numbly I nodded, said goodnight and walked through to the bedroom.

I don't remember much about that night either. The doctor must have come and given me something because I slept – unless I just passed out from emotional exhaustion.

When I woke, my watch told me it was six o'clock in the morning. I realised straight away where I was and then I remembered what had happened. The pain seemed to spread like volcanic lava, settling over me, round me, almost penetrating me. I couldn't shake it off, and felt as if I was suffocating underneath it. I must have cried out because the next minute Neil was there.

'Okay, okay, Helen, I've got you,' he said as I found myself in his arms for the third time in twenty-four hours.

'Oh, Neil, I felt as if I were suffocating!'

He gently released me. 'Do you want to come in the sitting room?'

'No, I'll be all right now.'

When he had left me, I drew back the heavy brocade curtains and sat on the window seat. It was just starting to get light and even at this early hour there were people already on the embankment below. Some were obviously going to work on early shift, others were running along the river, bitten by the fitness bug that had just become fashionable.

The pain had settled all over me as if it belonged there, as if it had a right to be there. And maybe it had. I tried to get my thoughts in some sort of order but couldn't. It was easier not to think at all. It was easier to act, to do something, so I did.

I bathed and dressed, then carefully, very carefully, put on my make-up and did my hair. I packed my suitcase and when I was ready I knocked gently on the sitting room door and went in. I got the feeling that Neil had never been asleep, but I said nothing.

He looked me over and smiled. 'Would you like to leave now?'

'Yes,' I said.

A car was waiting, parked outside the Strand entrance of the hotel. All I noticed about it was that it was not one of Peter's. Once we were out of the London traffic, past Hendon Way and onto the motorway, Neil put his foot down and we were soon eating up the miles.

'I realise this is probably insensitive,' Neil began, 'and not the right moment, but there's something I would really like to know and this is the last opportunity I'll ever have to ask you. If you can't

233

answer, or don't want to, I'll understand. I have ... I had ...' I realised he was nervous. He started again. 'I had known Peter for over twenty years. I thought I really knew him until he met you. Now I'm not sure I ever really understood him. How were you always so sure?''

'What do you mean?'

'Right from the beginning you seemed to have no doubts about him, your love for him, or his for you. How were you so sure?'

My mind unblanked. It suddenly became totally lucid. I sat back in the car seat, understanding the question and seeing the answer.

'It was that first night in Marbella. I knew him right at the beginning, that first night.'

Now it was Neil's turn to ask, 'What do you mean?'

'I saw the man he was that night – not the man he had to be. When I met him again, whatever was happening, I knew that man. I knew the playboy was not him. I knew the coldness and cruelty were not him. When I broke his cover it was almost a relief because then at last I began to understand that conflict. But even before, I never had any doubts that the man I had seen in Spain was the real Peter.'

'I don't know what you saw. I've never asked,' said Neil.

'One day, Neil, you may know.'

We fell silent for a while, then Neil said, 'Is there anything you want to ask me – any answers I may be able to give you?'

'Why can't you still be my friend?'

'The only way I could do that would be to come out of the Department myself, immediately. I gave Peter my word that I wouldn't do that. There are certain matters I have to bring to a conclusion. Then I think it would be too late.'

'Who will be the new Boss?' I asked, suddenly curious.

'No-one, Helen. Peter *was* the Department. There is no Department without him. It will now be merged into the official Intelligence Services. It's my job to do that and to make quite sure there's nothing left to show it ever existed. This is my final act of respect for him.'

'You worshipped him, didn't you?'

He looked a little surprised. 'Yes, I did. I would have died for him.'

'So would I. What am I going to do?' I cried out selfishly.

'Helen, I have something for you from him. I'm to give it to you when I leave. I suspect he'll tell you what to do. Would the man you knew in Spain have told you what to do?'

'Yes, he definitely would,' I said, feeling more sure.

It occurred to me at that moment that Neil must be hurting a lot too. He had been carrying out orders, a model of efficiency, yet he had just told me he worshipped Peter and no-one was concerned with his loss. Maybe he was as bereft as I was, and I wanted us to talk.

Soon we were outside my house.

'I'm not coming in,' he said abruptly. He came round and opened my door to let me out. 'But there's one thing—'

I interrupted him. 'Please, Neil,' I pleaded. 'Please come in and have some coffee with me.' Perhaps he saw my pain because, after looking at his watch, he relented.

'Right, but I have to leave at midday.'

He picked up my things and we went inside. I ushered him into the sitting room and when I returned with the coffee he was looking at the photographs of my children. I could see him closely studying the one

235

of my son, but he said nothing. I felt quite cold, so I put a match to the fire.

'Sit down.' I offered him a chair.

'No, not yet. I'm afraid there's something else I have to do. I have to ask you to give me the photographs you have of Peter.'

'No!' I almost shouted. I clutched the back of the chair. Neil waited, saying nothing. He knew he didn't have to; he knew me well enough to know that I would obey him because through him, I was still obeying Peter.

I let this new pain settle on top of all the rest.

'Wait here, I'll get them for you.'

I went upstairs for the photographs and found them at once. I took a deep breath, sat down on the bed and looked at them: first the one I had found at Jessie's when Peter was quite a young man, then the other, taken much later in London when I knew him. I noticed how much he had changed in the intervening years.

I tried to concentrate, to etch his face forever on my brain. But it was very hard to even look at him. I ran my finger over his features, over the steel-grey eyes, the aquiline nose, the strong chin and dimples.

Only when I was ready, which was quite some time, did I get up and go downstairs to Neil. He was still standing where I had left him. I handed him the photographs.

'Is there anything else you want?' I heard the hint of anger in my voice and it surprised me.

'I'm sorry, Helen.' He turned and, without looking at them, threw the photographs straight into the fire. I watched horrified as they shrivelled and burned in the flames. It was like a funeral pyre.

'I told you you wouldn't like what I had to do.' He put a large brown envelope on the table. 'That's from Peter. Now I must go.'

He walked out of the room, out of the house and out of my life. I never saw Neil again. Years later I realised it was the only way he could do it. At the time, what he did seemed brutal, callous and unnecessary. It left me angry but now I can see that was what he intended. Peter had given him instructions. Peter knew me and understood me very well. My anger knocked me out of the shock. It focused me and carried me through the next few days, exactly as it was meant to do.

Peter's sudden death; the necessity to immediately and completely close down all contacts with the Department; to burn the photographs – all this, coming at once, had the potential to destroy me.

Peter's death alone would have been enough.

Neil's behaviour that day was intended to make me angry. If I had been able to think straight then, I could have worked that out. Luckily I didn't. I was too close to it. I was hurting too much.

Peter knew me better than I knew myself. He knew that anger would be my best and only defence.

## Chapter 24
## Life

I kept looking at the large brown envelope. It was still on the table, exactly where Neil had placed it. Every so often I walked round it but I didn't pick it up. It fascinated me, even seduced me, but I couldn't pick it up. I was afraid of more pain. Something told me to leave it alone until I was ready. A voice inside said: 'Wait!'

So I left it lying there for three whole days. It almost became a person. I would circle it and talk to it. It became the focus of my anger and I wanted to throw it onto the fire. Sometimes I wondered if I was going mad. Then I would remember Peter had said to me the last time I saw him: 'You must regain your life. I will clear the way and give you everything you need to do so, but you must pick up what I give you – you will have to trust me. Eventually you will understand.'

On the fourth morning I knew I was ready for the envelope. Quietly, I sat down and tore it open. Inside were a tape, two sheets of paper and a small box covered in turquoise leather.

I opened the box first. Sitting on a velvet base was a heart-shaped diamond pendant set in white gold. I took it out and put it on, then went over to a mirror on the wall. It was quite, quite beautiful; very subtle, very real – very Peter. My fingers caressed it.

Sitting down again, I picked up the tape and looked at it – it was a recorded tape. On the label it said 'For Helen'. I put it down very quickly as if it was scalding my hand.

238

Next I picked up the two sheets of paper. There were no letter headings. On the first were the words Peter had read to me before he had said goodbye and I realised this was the piece of paper that had been tucked inside his copy of *A Tale of Two Cities*. On the bottom he had written: 'With apologies to Charles Dickens'.

The second sheet had three words on it – 'Ring Stuart Hamilton' – and a phone number. The name sprang out from the paper. It rang a bell but I couldn't place it; even though I sat there and desperately tried to remember, nothing came.

What I did know was that I couldn't ring him yet. Whoever he was, he would have to wait.

I will move quickly over the next few weeks. I don't want to dwell on the pain that hovered around me, waiting like a vulture to go in for the kill. I now knew how animals in the desert felt, abandoned and left alone to die. Suffice to say, I felt suicidal. Only two things stopped me from taking that fatal step. One was my children; the other was Peter's instructions. His words would not go away, nor would the piece of paper: 'Ring Stuart Hamilton.' The name definitely meant something but I still couldn't place it.

The tape remained on the table.

Eventually I was ready. I say that because I believe if you listen to yourself – I mean *really* listen and trust yourself – you will know when to move forward and when to stay still. Something quite powerful will tell you.

I waited until four o'clock in the afternoon then rang the number. There was no reply. That was okay. I had managed to dial the number. Now I knew I could do it again.

You need to understand that by this time there was no question of my trying to contact the Department or anyone in it. I had accepted that it was now closed for me – finished. Neil had made that very clear. He was right to do so and, looking back, I am grateful he did. Imagine the fruitless hours and pain involved if I had tried to make contact.

The tape was still on the table.

The next morning at exactly nine o'clock I tried the number again.

'Hello,' said a warm masculine voice.

'Is that Stuart Hamilton?'

A pause. 'Is that Helen?' The voice was like water in my desert.

'Yes,' I said.

'Where are you?'

'In Cheshire, where are you?'

'I'm in Hereford at the moment but if you tell me exactly where you are I can come to you. If you prefer to meet me somewhere we can arrange that.'

I wasn't used to a man who was so polite and considerate, or so eloquent. Men in the Department never used ten words when they could use two, especially Peter. I understood their clipped, precise style and was not quite sure how to handle such a different approach.

'Perhaps it would be better if you came here, if you don't mind,' I said.

'No, I don't mind at all. Right, it's nine o'clock now. I can be there by two o'clock. Is that okay?'

'Yes, fine.' I told him the address and gave him directions.

'Thank you. I'll see you at two o'clock then – goodbye.'

Suddenly it was all very formal. The phone clicked down. I still didn't remember who he was.

The tape called to me from the table.

I sat there, an animal curled up in the desert, but I knew someone was coming. Trust Peter and just wait. That was all I could do. I just wanted to stay still, to do nothing. I didn't prepare anything, didn't change my clothes or check my appearance. I just sat and waited. That for me was quite extraordinary. It showed where I was.

But what was I waiting for? Was it my saviour or my nemesis?

The tape called.

I had to play it before Stuart Hamilton arrived. After all, it could have instructions that impinged on whatever happened next. So I picked it up and walked unwillingly to the machine. I switched it on and clicked the tape into place.

Peter's voice came over. '*They told me what I must do.*' I clicked it off.

The sound of Peter's rich voice was almost too much to bear. I stood back. But I had to do it. I rewound the tape, pressed PLAY again. The voice sounded again. '*They told me what I must do.*' I clicked it off again.

You stupid girl, I thought. Pull yourself together. Use your training, use everything Peter taught you. Listen to the tape.

So I did.

Below is the tape transcript in full.

'*They told me what I must do. And I was faced at that moment with the realisation that I had stumbled onto something eminently precious. Something I was not prepared to lose. So I fought them. I argued, I cajoled, I threatened and I came near to pleading. After an hour they were still implacable. You were to be eliminated.*

'*I said I would resign. I told them where they could put their job. Gradually I wore them down. They agreed to the test, but on two conditions: I had to personally administer it, and if you failed, I would be personally responsible for killing you.*

'*I agreed to both.*

'*I was very angry. Angry because I had been fighting my*

knew I could never forget. I realised I could never again be free.

Don't think I'm complaining. If I could go back to that day, driving to Heathrow with Peter, and experience it all over again, knowing what I know, I would do it.

Why? Because of him. Because of Peter. I was immensely privileged to know and love this man. I was doubly privileged that my love was reciprocated.

But I still have a problem with one piece of the jigsaw puzzle. When I broke his cover, Peter obviously determined that this would never happen again. He immediately proceeded to weave such a tangled web around himself that he became the ultimate enigma.

I have never been able to confirm who he really was. Perhaps now only Sir Winston Churchill could enlighten us.

The last piece of the jigsaw puzzle simply does not fit. Perhaps it never should.

And perhaps the Department that doesn't exist should remain true to its name forever.